HOW TO
BUY &
SELL
YOUR HOME
without Getting
RIPPED **OFF!**

HOW TO
BUY&
SELL
YOUR HOME
without Getting
RIPPED OFF!

Patricia Boyd, CRA, CFS
Lonny Coffey

DEARBORN™
A **Kaplan Professional** Company

This publication is designed to provide accurate and authoritative information in regard to the subject matter covered. It is sold with the understanding that the publisher is not engaged in rendering legal, accounting, or other professional service. If legal advice or other expert assistance is required, the services of a competent professional should be sought.

Acquisitions Editor: Mary B. Good
Managing Editor: Jack Kiburz
Project Editor: Trey Thoelcke
Interior Design: Lucy Jenkins
Cover Design: Salvatore Concialdi
Typesetting: the dotted i

Printed in the United States of America

00 01 02 10 9 8 7 6 5 4 3 2 1

Library of Congress Cataloging-in-Publication Data
Boyd, Patricia, CFS.
   How to buy & sell your home without getting ripped off! / by Patricia Boyd & Lonny Coffey.
      p.   cm.
   Includes index.
   ISBN 0-7931-3706-3 (pbk.)
    1. House buying—United States—Handbooks, manuals, etc.   2. House selling—United States—Handbooks, manuals, etc.   I. Title: How to buy and sell your home without getting ripped off!.   II. Coffey, Lonny.   III. Title.
HD259.B68   1998
643'.12—dc21   99-089129

CONTENTS

PREFACE

When Patricia asked me to cowrite this book, I was excited. I always want to jump up on my soapbox and tell people what I think. When I entered the mortgage banking business in 1974, we were in a much simpler environment. Very few companies specialized in the origination of mortgage loans and fewer still in FHA (Federal Housing Administration) and VA (Department of Veterans Affairs) lending. Now anyone can get into the mortgage business overnight. If they operate in a state where mortgage lenders are not regulated, they can get into the business with no training, no expertise, and no money of their own.

The appetite for mortgage loans is so great that many times integrity is thrown out the window, at the expense of an uninformed consumer. There is no other industry that I know of that has such an open shot at the consumer as the mortgage industry. The answer is not more government regulation, but for educated consumers to know the warning signs so they can protect themselves from getting ripped off in the process of financing their new homes.

Our goal in writing this book is to bring you information that will help you make the correct choices in getting a mortgage for your new home.

—Lonny Coffey

ACKNOWLEDGMENTS

Special thanks to the following people for proofreading (over and over again!) and giving valuable feedback: Mike Boyd, Grady & Bonnie Watson, Rebekah Petrucci, Faye Buchholz, Shirley Watson, Cheri Glass, Evelyn Watson, Valery Savage, Charles & Linda Dahlheimer, Mary Daugherty, and Gene Eisman with Fannie Mae Public Relations.

A book is never written by one person. It takes a team to make it a reality.

INTRODUCTION

My experience has shown me that getting taken advantage of in the home buying and selling process occurs at all income levels and price ranges. It happens to those of all nationalities and age groups. It is time we put a stop to it. As the saying goes, *knowledge is power.* This book will give you the power to make educated financial decisions about your home and your future.

The real estate industry has such a bad reputation with the public that consumers do not know where to turn. Gallup surveys consistently rank the real estate industry at the bottom of the list of professions people distrust—just before car sellers and right after attorneys!

Why? Are all real estate agents and lenders unethical, dishonest, and greedy? As a 20-year veteran of the real estate and mortgage industry, I will give you a definite NO! There are a lot of professional, honest, hard-working people in the business.

The industry projects that in 2001 there will be $1.2 trillion worth of real estate sold in the United States through more than one million real estate agents, mortgage brokers, lenders, and loan officers. With that much money at stake, the industry attracts the good as well as the bad.

One of my goals as an educator is to help raise the image and level of service of the real estate industry to the public. I believe we can do this by changing the role of the real estate agent from a salesperson to a consumer real estate advocate (CRA), and by educating the consumer so that they can become a responsible team member. Decisions based on knowledge are less likely to become costly mistakes.

My goal for this book is to reach as many buyers and sellers as possible and educate you on how you can work in harmony with real estate professionals for a common goal—a successful closing.

A successful closing is one in which no one gets taken advantage of and everyone leaves the transaction with long lasting professional relationships in place. The result—increased home ownership and fewer foreclosures!

—Patricia Boyd

CHAPTER ONE

Building an Accountable Real Estate Team

Welcome to the wonderful world of real estate! In this chapter you will learn how to build a team that you can depend on to protect you from "getting ripped off" when you are buying or selling real estate. Identify major players and their roles. Take a behind-the-scenes look with each one so that you will know how to select the players for your team. Industry trends, terminology, and procedures are explained in a language you can understand so that you can build your team with confidence. After reading this chapter, you will be able to

- communicate effectively as you build your real estate team.

- ask intelligent questions and understand the answers.

- know whom to turn to when there is something you do not understand.

- get a good night's sleep, knowing that you are too well informed to be taken advantage of easily!

Five Major Trends Revolutionizing the Real Estate Industry

Many of you are probably aware that the real estate industry is in the midst of a revolution. You may think you know how to buy and sell real estate because you bought a home a few years ago. With the major changes that have been taking place in the field nationwide, however, that may not be the case. Even those in the business full time must make a commitment to continuing education. Keeping informed of the changes in the marketplace is the only way to stay on the leading edge and provide quality service. You should question everyone you consider for your team about their strategies to stay current.

The five major trends in this revolution are

1. technology,

2. desktop underwriting,

3. B & C lending (loans made to borrowers with less-than-perfect credit),

4. credit scoring, and

5. computerized loan origination services (CLOs).

This book will show you how to make these trends work for you instead of against you. Then you can share the new vision of the real estate and mortgage industry of the new millennium. The focus is on the consumer. The hard sell approach to selling is replaced with a consumer friendly one and feeling good about who you are and what you do.

Real estate agents and loan officers work in harmony with a service team to serve the customer. The result is long-term productive relationships between consumers, REALTORS®, lenders, appraisers, title companies, and closing agents. Everyone makes more money and feels good about who they are and what they do.

Remember Physical Education (PE) in elementary school? When it came time to play a game, team captains were selected. The team captain's responsibility was to select a team that would help win the game. Choosing players who would give 100 percent was very important.

When you decide to be involved in real estate, why leave the players on your team to chance? Take charge by becoming your own team captain and selecting a team that will help you get the results you want.

MAJOR PLAYERS

The first step is learning about each part of the game and understanding each player's role. This chapter will give you a look at five major players you may want to have on your real estate team:

1. Real estate agents

2. Lenders

3. Appraisers

4. Title companies

5. Closing agents

The more you understand about what goes on behind the scenes, the easier it will be to keep each member accountable for premium quality service.

Real Estate Agents

For the best results, you must take the time to understand the services a real estate agent can provide for you and carefully select the agent you want to work with. A professional real estate agent can counsel you on the steps involved in buying or selling real estate in his or her market area.

The good news is that a new day is dawning in real estate with a new breed of real estate agent leading the way. They have been there all along; they are just getting easier to find.

Bob McKinnon, past president of Century 21 in the Northwest and a 28-year veteran of the real estate industry, calls this new breed *real estate careerists,* people who are getting into real estate to build a career, not to make a fast buck.

Today there are more trustworthy real estate agents in the business than ever before. Honesty, trust, dependability, and quality service are their top priorities. But beware! There are still the wheeler-dealers out there too! They just are not as successful as they use to be.

Your first step in selecting an agent is to understand the role your real estate agent plays. A real estate agent must be licensed by the state in which he or she works and must be associated with a licensed broker. The broker assumes responsibility for the agents' actions and is considered to "hold" the license for the agent during the time they work together. In most states, an agent must serve a specified amount of time as a licensed agent, attend additional training, and pass a test before they can receive their brokers license.

An agent with a broker's license may work for a broker as an independent contractor or may open an office as an independent broker.

Independent Contractors

Most real estate agents are independent contractors. They are self-employed, even though they may be affiliated with and work in a specific broker's office. They are paid on commission, must pay all of their own expenses, and do not receive insurance or retirement benefits.

Is a real estate agent worth their commission? This question often comes up. The answer is that a *professional, knowledgeable,* and *trustworthy* agent is definitely worth the commission. Especially when you consider that they offer a 100 percent guarantee on their services. If they do not bring sellers an acceptable contract or find buyers a home they want to buy, the agent does not get paid. In other words, the agent does not get paid until after a transaction closes, the seller receives the money, and the buyer gets the home! How many professionals offer you those kinds of terms?

Consider that unless an agent owns a real estate company or works in an office and pays the broker a monthly desk fee for the services the broker provides, the commission is usually split with the broker. If the broker is affiliated with a large franchise such as RE/MAX or Century 21, a percentage also is taken for franchise fees. Commission splits vary depending on experience and productivity.

Most listing agents also agree to list the house in the Multiple Listing Service (MLS). That means that agents from all real estate companies can show the listing and bring offers on the house. If an agent other than the listing agent sells the house, the commission is split with the selling agent.

The commission fee for selling a home varies nationwide and from agent to agent. To give you an idea of a typical commission, use a 50/50 split between the broker and the agent and a commission fee of 8 percent (which may be lower in some areas and higher in others) for the following example:

Sales price:	$100,000
Commission:	× 8%
	$ 8,000
Listing office commission:	$ 4,000
Selling office commission:	$ 4,000
Broker split:	$ 2,000
Agent split:	$ 2,000

Does $2,000 sound like a lot of money for the individual agent or broker to receive from a transaction? Before you answer, consider that the broker has to pay expenses for an office, such as rent, utilities, phones, advertising, franchise fees, MLS fees, signs, training, secretaries, computers, copy machines, recruiting, insurance on the office, taxes, errors & omission insurance, etc.

Most states also require brokers to renew their license every two years by attending a seminar with continuing education credits and to pay renewal fees. Most real estate agents also have to renew their license every two years with continuing education courses and renewal fees. They also pay all of their own expenses.

Every listing and every buyer an agent works with costs money when you consider the time invested, marketing materials used, and expenses for gas and mileage on the car. Unfortunately for real estate professionals, every transaction does not result in a closing. This may be due to buyers and sellers changing their minds, the loan being rejected, market conditions, or simply that a buyer purchased a home through a different agent or from a for sale by owner (FSBO) or the seller listed with another agent.

A member of the new breed—the real estate careerist that is knowledgeable, trustworthy, and professional—*could actually save you money.* A knowledgeable agent can counsel you on financing and marketing techniques that can help you keep more money in your pocket, not in someone else's!

Finding the Right Real Estate Agent

How do you go about finding this new breed? It has been said that one of the greatest challenges for consumers today is finding top professionals to counsel them on personal and financial matters. Whether you are looking for an attorney, doctor, financial planner, or real estate agent, you should take the time to interview them before making a commitment to work with them.

Many times buyers and sellers simply call an ad out of the paper or walk into a real estate office and work with whomever happens to be available. If they are not happy with the services of that agent, they go to another office, then another and another.

Even worse, they may just work with the first agent they encounter, not realizing that their choice of agent could have a significant impact on the end result of the transaction.

The real estate agent is one of the most important members of your team. Take the time to find an agent who can meet your needs and make your home buying or selling experience a successful one. Asking questions up front will save you time and money in the long run. A list of questions has been provided at the end of this section to help you get started.

Let the agent know right up front that you are interviewing real estate agents because you are a serious buyer or seller (or both). It is important to you that you both know what to expect from each other.

Put together a list of prospective agents to interview by asking for referrals from friends and family. You also may want to ask other professionals in the real estate industry for recommendations. Title company representatives and closers may be especially helpful because they work closely with many agents and will know the type of service and professionalism each provides.

You also can check on the Internet for individuals' Web sites and for designation groups that offer referral programs. For example, the Residential Financing Council (RFC) will list every Certified Finance Specialist (CFS) in the group. Its Web site is located at www.rfcouncil.com.

Agency

In the past, agents were legally bound to represent sellers because the seller was paying the commission. In recent years, *buyer agency* or *buyer representative* has become popular. Most states now require a written agency disclosure form be signed up front that clearly spells out whom the agent will be representing. Some companies exclusively offer buyer agency. This means they do not list homes for sellers and only work with buyers.

Dual agency means an agent represents both the buyer and the seller in a transaction and the agent must take a neutral position if the buyer wants to make an offer on a home that the agent's company has listed. Some people feel that this is not in the best interest of the consumer. Many times the critical stage in homebuying is during the offer and negotiation of the sales price. Buyers should have an advocate in their corner looking out for their best interest.

Beyond the agency relationship, some believe agents also should provide "due diligence." In addition to finding and showing property to buyers, they also should do a property value study, help with home inspections, refer qualified mortgage professionals and real estate attorneys, and advise on any environmental hazards in the area. If they do not provide these services they are not performing "due diligence."[1]

Charles Dahlheimer, president of Professional Certification Corporation and a noted author and lecturer, cofounded REBAC (Real Estate Buyer's Agent Council) in 1992. He believes that consumers need professional representation when buying a home. Members of REBAC receive special training in buyer representation and are designated as Accredited Buyer Representatives. REBAC's *Accredited Buyer Representative (ABR®)* designation has become the benchmark of excellence in buyer representation and has become the official buyer agency designation of the National Association of REALTORS®.

Dahlheimer also believes that financing is a critical part of the process in buying and selling real estate and has recently cofounded the *Residential Financing Council* and the *Certified Finance Specialist (CFS)* designation. CFS designees receive advanced training in financing residential real estate and are uniquely qualified to help buyers and sellers save time and money through their knowledge of financing options.

The National Association of REALTORS® (NAR)

The National Association of REALTORS® (NAR), founded in 1908, is the nation's largest professional trade association. NAR supports such issues as affordable housing, equal opportunity for home ownership, private property protection, prevention of real estate fraud, preservation of the right to deduct mortgage interest from individual income taxes, and many others.

"REALTOR®" identifies real estate agents who are members of the National Association of REALTORS®. All state-licensed real estate

---

[1]Pat Rioux, *Secrets to Getting the Best Agent,* International Real Estate Digest.

agents are not REALTORS®. A REALTOR® pays annual dues to NAR and also is a member of a state association of REALTORS®. They must abide by NAR's Code of Ethics and pledge to serve all parties in real estate transactions fairly.

There are no right or wrong answers to the following questions. You are simply asking questions that will help you know what to expect from the agent you commit to work with. You also should let the agent know what they can expect from you.

QUESTIONS TO ASK YOUR REAL ESTATE AGENT

- How long have you been in real estate?

- Are you a member of the National Association of REALTORS®?

- What did you do before you got into real estate?

- What designations do you have?

- How will the training you received for those designations help me with my real estate needs?

- How do you stay current with your designations?

- Do you represent buyers, sellers, or both?

- How do you handle dual agency?

- Do you have a team of lenders, title insurers, and closing agents you work with?

- Why do you work with the particular team you use?

- How much time do you have to work with me?

(continued)

- Do you have a list of references that I can call?

- Do you specialize in any particular type of properties or in certain areas or territories?

- Is it currently a seller's market or a buyer's market? (A seller's market means there are fewer houses on the market than buyers in the marketplace. A buyer's market means there are fewer buyers in the market and an abundance of houses for sale.)

- Are you up to date with current real estate financing options?

- How long have you lived in this area?

- If you work with assistants, who will I be working with the most—the assistant or you?

- If the assistant will be working with me most of the time, what are the assistant's background and qualifications?

- What day(s) do you take off?

- Do you have vacation scheduled during the time I will be working with you? (You should not mind for them to take vacation while working with you as long as you are kept informed and have someone else to work with.)

- If something unexpected comes up, do you have someone who covers for you?

Lenders

You have many sources for obtaining loans these days. You can shop for loans in your local marketplace through banks, mortgage companies, or credit unions; make loan application by telephone with a lender in another state; or search for loans on the Internet. It really can get confusing, but it does not have to be if you take the time to become educated and, whenever possible, work with one of the lenders on your agent's team. Your agent brings them repeat business and this can make the difference in the level of service you receive.

Some agents are afraid to refer lenders. They fear that if something goes wrong they will be blamed. That could be true in some cases, but successful agents realize that referrals are an important part of the real estate industry.

Buyers and sellers look to their agents for advice on what is needed to complete a transaction. They expect agents to be aware of who is known for giving the best service in the business.

The lender you select to work with is critical to the success of your team. Understanding their business, the rules and regulations they must adhere to, and the process through which they send loan applications will ensure you make it to closing much faster and easier.

The Mortgage Business

The first step to understanding the mortgage business is to understand where the money for mortgages comes from. Loans are originated in the *primary market* by lenders in your local area. To free up more money to originate new loans, the *primary market lenders* usually sell their loans to *secondary market investors*.

Thus, two markets supply the money for real estate transactions:

1. Primary market—comprised of lenders in your local market that originate loans

2. Secondary market—a nationwide market in which investors buy and sell loans backed by real estate

Players in the secondary market include:

- Fannie Mae—Federal National Mortgage Association (FNMA)

- Freddie Mac—Federal Home Loan Mortgage Corporation (FHLMC)

- Insurance companies

- Private investors

- Commercial banks

- Savings and loan institutions

Fannie Mae is a federally chartered, shareholder owned, and privately managed mortgage corporation.

Congress chartered Freddie Mac, the nation's second largest source of funds, to promote the flow of funds into the housing market. It provides an outlet for lenders to sell their conventional loans.

The secondary market serves two important functions for the real estate industry:

1. It promotes investment in real estate by making funds available for real estate loans.

2. It provides a measure of stability in the primary market by moderating the effects of real estate cycles.

The secondary market sets guidelines the primary market must abide by if they want to sell loans they originate. These guidelines will be discussed in Chapter 3.

Primary market lenders sell loans to the secondary market so that they have more money to generate new loans. If the secondary market did not exist, the local primary lenders would be limited in the number of loans they could originate and fewer people could obtain financing for their homes.

While there are other sources for obtaining mortgage loans, the following are the three types of primary lenders you will deal with most often:

1. A *mortgage broker:*

    - Originates loans.
    - Brokers loans to mortgage lenders.

- Does not use its own funds to close the loan.
- Cannot portfolio (portfolio means to keep the loan in-house and not sell it to the secondary market).

2. A *banker:*

- Originates loans.
- Also can broker to other lenders.
- Usually closes loans in its own name.
- Can portfolio (keep the loan in-house).

3. A *mortgage banker:*

- Originates loans.
- Can broker loans to outside investors.
- Can use own funds to close loans.
- Cannot portfolio.

Mortgage brokers are just what their name implies; they broker loans to bankers or mortgage bankers. They do not have (in most cases) FHA or VA approval and are not approved seller servicers with Fannie Mae or Freddie Mac. Although there are some reputable brokers in the industry, some people feel that brokers take the professionalism of the mortgage industry down to the level of people working out of their garages, with no net worth or expertise in the business.

In some states someone, who literally could have been unemployed with no practical experience in lending, could hang a sign out and put an ad in the paper and *poof* they are a mortgage lender that you assume has credibility. The good news is that steps are being taken to require licensing in a lot of states. Texas, for example, started requiring licensing in January 2000.

In general, brokers may have a harder time providing a quality level of service than others in that they are in fact middlemen. They generally do not have in-house underwriters, closers, etc. If you are putting extra people in the process, it can slow down the process. There are always exceptions to the rule and the key is to take the time to be an informed consumer. Which brings us to the next step, interviewing lenders.

A good loan officer is worth his or her weight in gold! The following questions will give you a place to start; be sure to add your own questions to this list as you think of them.

QUESTIONS TO ASK LENDERS

- Are you a mortgage banker or a broker?

- What loan programs do you have available?

- What down payment options are available?

- What is your prequalifying/preapproval procedure?

- What is your turnaround time for loan approval?

- Are any fees paid up front at loan application?

- If there are fees, what do they cover and how much are they? Are they negotiable?

- Will you give me the APR[2] and a good faith estimate to compare with other lenders?

- What are current interest rates?

- Will you be available by phone or in person on the day of closing?

- What is your lock-in procedure? (Most lenders offer a buyer the option to lock in the interest rate at loan application or to "float" the rate and lock in closer to closing if the buyer thinks rates may come down. A 60-day lock is usually free but you may have to pay a fee for longer lock-in periods if you will not close within 60 days. Make sure you get the

[2]The annual percentage rate (APR) is the interest rate and the closing cost paid the first year. Lenders charging higher fees can be identified by their higher APRs.

lock-in agreement in writing. See Chapter 2 for more details on locking in.)

- Do you have a source of loans for borrowers with credit problems (if applicable to your situation)?

- Does your company have a policy to contact me in writing if anything changes after I have received my *good faith estimate* of closing costs?

- Is your only business hard credit (subprime) loans or do you also offer FHA, VA, and conventional loans?

- Does your company allow loan officers to take rate overages?

An *overage* is the amount of discount charged over the amount the lender is actually charging for that day. Most lenders set a minimum fee that their loan officers must charge for interest rates. The loan officer then can charge an amount over that to make a higher commission. A loan officer does not make as much on a loan as an agent does on a sale. Most lenders pay a percentage of the origination fee—somewhere around 50 percent or 50 basis points. On a $100,000 loan that is only $500. The loan officer can add to the minimum discount required by charging an overage. Factors that influence the amount the loan officer's charge include:

- Competition with other lenders

- Their reputation for performing as they say they will

Loan officers who always get the job done on time may be able to charge fees higher than other loan officers because of the confidence the buyer, seller, and agents have in getting the loan closed. The importance of integrity really can be an issue here. If you go to an unethical lender and do not compare rates and services, you may be charged a lot more for your loan than you would have if you used a lender on your agent's team.

LENDER COMPARISON CHART

Lender Comparison Chart

Date	Lender	Contact	Phone	Loan	Lock	Fees	APR

Conventional, FHA, and VA loans are priced differently, so be sure to get a quote on all three types or state the loan you are interested in if you already know which type you want. The length of time the rate can be locked in is usually quoted for 10 days, 30 days, or 60 days to process a file. Make sure you are comparing lenders' quotes for the same lock-in period.

When comparing lenders' fees and loan programs, you may want to use a chart similar to the Lender Comparison Chart to help you compare "apples to apples." Keep in mind that integrity and reputation are as important as price.

Also make sure you are comparing lenders' quotes for the same type of loans with the same lock-in period. Interest rates usually are quoted on 10-day, 30-day, or 60-day lock-in periods. A lender may sound like it has the best price, but it is quoting a 10-day lock-in price (you have to close in 10 days), while the others are quoting 60-day lock-in pricing, which gives you more time to process and close your loan.

Appraisers

An appraiser is someone qualified to estimate the value of real property. The appraisal is the written estimate or opinion of value from an appraiser, based on similar properties that are on the market and that have sold recently in the area. The lender qualifies the property as well as the borrower. The property is the security for the loan. Lenders also have appraisal guidelines they must meet if they want to sell the loan in the secondary market.

One issue that always comes up is the buyer's right to the appraisal. Section 223 (d), section 701 (e), of the FDIC Improvement Act Public Law (PL) 102-242 of the Equal Credit Opportunity Act (ECOA) reads:

> *"Each creditor shall promptly furnish to an applicant upon written request by an applicant made within a reasonable period of time of the application, a copy of the appraisal report used in connection with the applicant's application for a loan that is or would be secured by a lien on residential property.*
>
> *The creditor may require the applicant to reimburse the creditor for the cost of the appraisal."*

The last statement usually is not very meaningful because, in most states, the buyer pays for the appraisal anyway. In the past, when sellers listed their house they could order an appraisal to help determine value. Then that appraisal could be used when their buyer made loan application.

That practice is not in effect anymore because the guidelines now state that the lender making the loan must be the client of the appraiser. In other words, the lender has to order the appraisal that will be used to determine the value of the property.

This change was made to help prevent fraud and to ensure that the collateral for the loan—the property—was sufficient to cover the loan in the event of foreclosure.

A seller still can order an appraisal to help set the price for the property. That appraisal just cannot be used for a buyer's loan application.

Avoiding Appraisal Problems

One way to avoid problems with appraisals is for the seller to make sure to price the home correctly before putting it on the market. The buyer also should be sure not to offer more than the home will appraise for. The easiest way to do this is to have a real estate professional prepare a *market evaluation* (also referred to as a *competitive market analysis*) for you.

A professional real estate agent will use an approach similar to an appraiser when preparing a market evaluation to determine the range of value for a home. The agent usually will not charge you for this service as long as you consider working with them when buying or selling real estate.

The market evaluation will compare similar homes in a neighborhood. It will show:

- Homes currently on the market

- Homes that have sold in the past six months

- Homes listed that did not sell (expired listings)

Your real estate professional also should be able to give you information on homes that have sold but not closed (pending sales), and be able to update you on the current condition of the market. For example, a seller's market refers to a market where there are more buyers than there are houses available for sale. A buyer's market means there are fewer buyers available and a surplus of houses.

Pricing a house right in the beginning is the smartest way for a seller to get the best price for the home. History has shown that overpriced homes help sell the competition. When buyers see the overpriced home and then see a similar home priced lower, they feel they are getting a good deal and quickly make an offer on the lower priced home.

You also will find that the longer a house is on the market, the less the seller is likely to get for it. When buyers see that a home has been on the market for a while unsold, they feel they have more leverage to negotiate. They also may fear there is something wrong with the house because no one has bought it.

Sellers also can avoid problems with appraisals by doing a walk-through of the property with their real estate agent. A good agent can point out items that will affect the appraisal that could be repaired by the seller before the house is put on the market. (See the *FHA/VA Appraiser Checklist* at the end of this section.)

As Barb Schwartz, a talented real estate educator and author says, "Buyers remember what they see, not what will be." The same holds true for appraisers. Appraisers can make or break a deal. The more you understand about the appraisal process, the easier it will be for you to prevent problems.

Most good real estate agents and loan officers are familiar with the appraisers in their area and have added one or more to their team.

Types of Appraisers

Like sales associates, appraisers obtain designations that reflect their professional status and experience. The highest appraiser designations are both earned from the *Appraisal Institute* at:

875 North Michigan Avenue
Chicago, IL 60611
(312) 296-4447

The designations the Appraisal Institute offers are:

• Member Appraisal Institute (MAI)

• Senior Residential Appraiser (SRA)

Appraisers can be independent appraisers (self-employed) or in-house appraisers (employed by a lender).

Lender Approved Processing Program (LAPP)

Some lenders also have LAPP approval from the VA. This means that because a lender's underwriter can underwrite the appraisal rather than send it to the VA for underwriting, it can process a VA loan faster than a lender without LAPP approval.

FHA now requires a disclosure to be signed called, "For Your Protection: Get a Home Inspection." This form must be signed before the buyer signs a contract with the seller. Appraisers now have more work to do with an FHA appraisal so they may be taking longer than conventional or VA appraisals and the price may be higher.

Drive-By Appraisals

Fannie Mae and Freddie Mac have approved "drive-by" appraisals. The appraiser does not physically visit the property, but establishes value from information obtained from a computer bank. These appraisals are usually less expensive and are used with Fannie Mae's Desktop Underwriter and Freddie Mac's Loan Prospector underwriting programs.

The Appraisal Checklist highlights the major items an appraiser may consider. Sellers should use the checklist to evaluate their home prior to putting it on the market. Buyers who plan to use FHA or VA financing programs should consider the criteria before making a final choice. Buyers and sellers should know, however, that using this list does not guarantee an appraisal will be accepted by the lender.

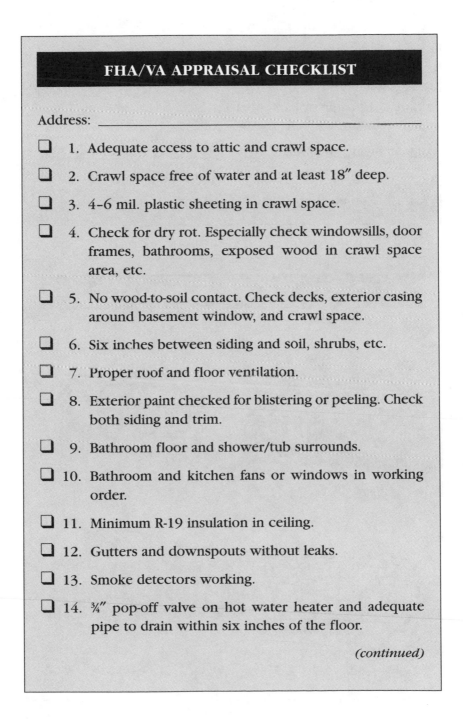

FHA/VA APPRAISAL CHECKLIST

Address: _____

❑ 1. Adequate access to attic and crawl space.

❑ 2. Crawl space free of water and at least 18″ deep.

❑ 3. 4–6 mil. plastic sheeting in crawl space.

❑ 4. Check for dry rot. Especially check windowsills, door frames, bathrooms, exposed wood in crawl space area, etc.

❑ 5. No wood-to-soil contact. Check decks, exterior casing around basement window, and crawl space.

❑ 6. Six inches between siding and soil, shrubs, etc.

❑ 7. Proper roof and floor ventilation.

❑ 8. Exterior paint checked for blistering or peeling. Check both siding and trim.

❑ 9. Bathroom floor and shower/tub surrounds.

❑ 10. Bathroom and kitchen fans or windows in working order.

❑ 11. Minimum R-19 insulation in ceiling.

❑ 12. Gutters and downspouts without leaks.

❑ 13. Smoke detectors working.

❑ 14. ¾″ pop-off valve on hot water heater and adequate pipe to drain within six inches of the floor.

(continued)

❑ 15. Roof inspection by licensed roofer if three-year life is questionable.

❑ 16. 100 amp. minimum electrical service. 200 amp. minimum with electric heat.

❑ 17. Woodstove/wall heater as only heat source is acceptable only in homes of 900 sq. ft. or less.

❑ 18. Zoning appropriate for anticipated use.

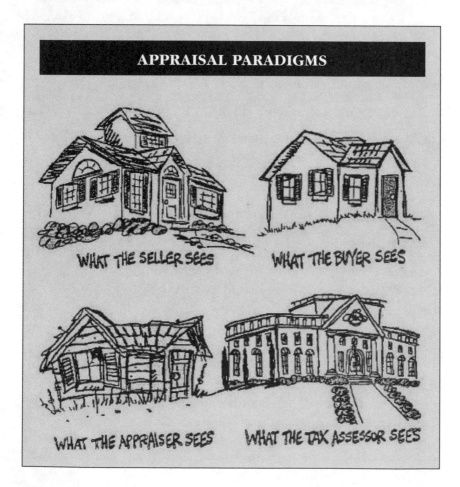

APPRAISAL PARADIGMS

WHAT THE SELLER SEES

WHAT THE BUYER SEES

WHAT THE APPRAISER SEES

WHAT THE TAX ASSESSOR SEES

Title Companies

Title companies assist the buyer and the lender with the legal aspects of transferring clear title to a property. Your title company also will be a good source to ask for referrals to qualified real estate agents and lenders in your area.

Contrary to popular opinion, all title companies are not created equal. While the fees for their services may be the same, the level of service they provide can vary greatly.

Understanding the Title Process

Title is "the legally recognized evidence of a person's right to possess property." A title insurance policy protects against loss or damage to title.

The title insurance policy usually is subject to exclusions, terms, exceptions, and provisions in the policy. Defects that are not covered should be spelled out in the policy. A buyer should be sure to read it carefully and ask for an explanation on anything not understood.

In some areas an *abstract of title* is obtained instead of a title policy. The abstract is a history of recorded interest in the property. The abstract usually is reviewed by an attorney who gives his or her opinion of the condition of title. The abstract is not a title—it is only a record of what has been recorded. It also does not judge the correctness of the items it lists. Abstracts do not protect the owner against undiscovered defects in title, so many buyers prefer the title policy.

It is a good idea to get a *preliminary title report* on the property as soon as possible. If there are any clouds, liens, or judgments on the property, it may take some time to clear the title.

The two most common types of insurance policies are the *standard policy* and the *extended policy.*

After searching public records the title company will issue a standard policy. The homebuyer may purchase an extended coverage policy. This policy could include coverage for defects apparent from inspection and unrecorded easements or mechanics' liens. A mechanic's lien is a charge filed against a property declaring the property security for the payment of a debt for work done and/or materials furnished.

For example, the unpaid roofer filed a mechanic's lien against a property. After he was paid and the lien was satisfied, clear title was given to the buyer.

If a debt is found that is secured by the property, the title company will protect against loss by agreeing to pay the lien or to defend against the claim. The policy will not provide coverage unless there is an actual loss or protect against problems created, assumed, or agreed to by the insured.

What Can Make a Title Defective?

- *Human error.* Errors in copying, indexing, or recording; errors by administrators, executors, trustees, guardians, or attorneys; destruction of records

- *Fraud.* Illegal acts of attorneys, guardians, trustees, or administrators

- *Liens and other rights.* Unpaid income, property, estate, or gift taxes; homestead rights or community property rights; irregular court proceedings, court opinion reversals, or lack of court jurisdiction; defective foreclosures

- *Improper deeds and wills.* Deeds by persons of unsound mind or by minors; deeds delivered after death or without the grantor's consent; invalid, suppressed, or erroneous will; missing heirs; unsettled estates

Owner's Policies and Lender's Policies

A premium is paid at the time the insured document is recorded. Deciding who pays for the policy is negotiable between the buyer and the seller. Usually the seller pays for the *owner's policy* for the new owners (the buyers).

The owner's policy continues for as long as the insured has an interest in the property or has liability because of a prior interest. The buyer usually pays for *lender's policy,* which covers the property for the life of the loan.

Tips for Working with Title Companies

- Use full legal names of parties when preparing the contract. Include addresses, and home and work telephone numbers for the seller, buyer, and agents involved.

- Provide title company with a copy of seller's title policy whenever possible.

- When the order for the title report is submitted, inform the title company of any liens, bankruptcies, divorces, law suits, improvement liens, mechanics' liens, etc.

- Furnish marital status of all parties at time the purchase and sale contract is turned in to the title company.

QUESTIONS TO ASK TITLE COMPANIES

- What services do you provide?

- Do you have an escrow (closing) department?

- Do you give discounts on title policies if a seller has purchased one in the past three years on the subject property?

- May I have a copy of your fee schedule?

- Who receives a copy of the title policy?

- How soon is the policy available after a buyer makes loan application?

- Do you charge cancellation fees if the deal falls through?

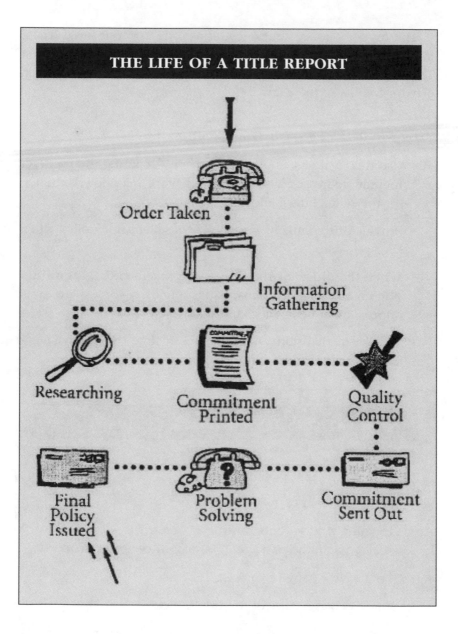

Closing Agents

The *closing agent,* also called an *escrow agent,* usually is chosen in advance and written into the sales contract. Escrow usually is opened with a lawyer, a title company, or an escrow company. In some areas, the real estate agent may perform escrow.

Escrow is the process in which money and documents are held by a disinterested third party—called a *closing agent* or an *escrow agent*—until certain conditions have been met. The purpose of escrow is to help ensure that the transfer of property ownership occurs fairly and legally. Opening escrow simply means taking the sales contract and earnest money and depositing them with the company that is handling escrow.

There must be an agreement in writing and a deposit made before escrow can be opened. This can be done by anyone in the transaction, but it is most often done by the agent or the loan officer.

Understanding the Escrow Process

The closing agent's role is to make sure the buyer and seller perform as they agreed to in the sales agreement. Because a closing agent is not affected by the outcome of the transaction, there is less risk of fraud or violation of the terms of the agreement.

A closing agent is responsible for

- holding and disbursing funds according to instructions.

- clearing the title according to the sales agreement.

- preparing documents necessary for the transaction.

- preparing final closing documents and closing statements.

- securing payoff demands and beneficiary statements from existing lenders and requesting full reconveyances of any deeds of trust to be paid off in escrow.

- recording the necessary documents when all conditions of the transaction have been met.

- coordinating closing, disbursement of funds, and paperwork between buyer, seller, real estate agents, lenders, and attorneys.

A closing agent is not responsible for

- writing sales agreements or addendums.

- negotiating disputes or terms between principals.

- giving legal advice.

- deciding who is right or wrong in a dispute.

- releasing earnest money without permission from all parties involved.

When the buyer receives loan approval, the lender's closing department will submit instructions for closing to the closing (escrow) agent. If the approval included conditions from the underwriter, the instructions will require that all conditions be met at closing before the escrow company is allowed to fund.

Other items that are specified in the instructions include:

- The loan documents must be executed by the buyer.

- The title insurance in the amount of the loan must be issued to insure the lender's interest.

- The title policy must show only those exceptions approved by the lender.

- Fire insurance must be issued for at least the amount of the loan, with the lender named as loss payee.

- Fees for all inspections and repairs must be collected.

Problems can cause delays. If there have been changes made from the original instructions, such as the date of closing occurring after the date on which the sales contract money has expired, amendments or extensions must be drawn up and signed by all parties. Other problems that cause delays include:

- *Seller* could have delinquent taxes, possible foreclosure, federal tax liens, judgments, payoffs, or additional costs on second liens.

- *Property* could have remodeling performed without permits; septic system problems; liability for the cost or extent of repairs, such as severe infestation or dry rot; a roof that is expected to last less than five years or has a heavy accumulation of moss; or health department certificates for water systems.

- *Buyer* could have child support or divorce judgments; or problems with possession date, power of attorney, or conditions that need to be met for underwriting.

It is important that the sales contract is specific regarding instructions for possession and prorations. The buyer and seller think of closing as the date they sign the documents. Closing is actually the date the deed is recorded and funds have been disbursed. This could be 24 to 72 hours after signing.

Most people try to close at the end of the month so they can pay less prorated interest on the loan, thus reducing their cost required for closing. Many times loan approval comes in at the last minute and documents are rushed to escrow. Then the pressure is on the escrow company to get the loans already scheduled closed and funded in addition to all the last-minute "rush" loans. Needless to say, mortgage and escrow companies can be a madhouse at the end of every month.

One way to reduce a lot of stress is to try to close by the third week of the month before the rush starts. There is a misconception by many that it costs you more not to close at the end of the month. The day you close, you pay interest from that day through the end of the month. The days that have passed are the seller's responsibility and will be credited to you at closing. Calculate your daily interest as follows:

Loan amount × Interest rate ÷ 365 × Number of days left in month
$100,000 × 8% = $8,000 ÷ 365 = $21.91 (daily interest) × 15 (days)
= $328.

If you closed your loan on January 15, your first payment would be due March 1. If you closed your loan the last day of January, you would pay no interest and your first payment would be due March 1. As you can see, you are paying interest only for the days you actually own the home.

There is a common practice in some states called *short pay*. That is where your loan actually funds in the first few days of the month and you do not pay interest but you actually receive an interest credit on your closing statement (also called the HUD 1).

Let us say you closed on a short pay on February 4 and receive an interest credit for four days. Your first payment would still be due March 1. So you see, you are never going to pay more or less money; you are just going to pay for the days you own the home.

Closing no later than the third week of the month is also a good idea for sellers who have an underlying FHA loan on their property. FHA requires interest to be paid for the entire month regardless of the closing date. The catch is that the underlying lender must receive the pay-off funds by the end of the month. If you wait until the last week to sign and close, the funds may not get to the lender until after the first of the next month. In that case, a full month of interest would be due.

Power of Attorney

If one of the parties involved must be out of town when it is time to close, be sure to have a power of attorney recorded when escrow is opened or as soon as the situation comes up. The power of attorney grants a specific person the right to sign on behalf of another. The escrow company can prepare the necessary paperwork and explain what is involved.

A general power of attorney grants the right to sign all documents, no matter what kind, during a person's absence. A specific power of attorney specifies exactly what may be signed. Most closing agents prefer to prepare the power of attorney in advance of closing so that if a problem occurs it can be cleared up before the closing date.

The power of attorney is recorded with the county recorder. It can be canceled when the person returns by recording a cancellation of the power at the recorder's office. The death of the person granting the power of attorney or of the person receiving the power of attorney automatically cancels it.

If you have a transaction using a power of attorney, it is a good idea to check with the lender to make sure there are no special requirements. For example, some lenders require that the title company verify that the person not present at the closing (the one the power of attorney is for) be contacted by phone to verify he or she is still alive.

In most cases this would not be a problem. But what happens if the person in question is in the navy and on a ship in the middle of the ocean somewhere? Making sure everyone involved is aware of the situation in advance solves most problems that may come up.

Closing and Funding

The normal time for escrow can be from 30 to 60 days, depending on the turnaround time for loan approval and when the clients wish to close. It is a good idea for the buyer to inspect the property one last time before closing to check on the condition of the property and on personal property items that are to remain.

The procedure for signing the documents varies across the country. In some areas, the buyer and seller go in at the same time to sign. In other areas, the buyer goes in first and the seller goes in second. The buyers usually are required to have a certified check or money order for the closing costs. If the closing costs are slightly higher, the closing agent may allow a personal check for the difference. If the amount is less, the closing agent can reimburse the buyer with a check. It is a good idea for the buyers to find out the closing agent's policy before obtaining the check or money order.

Before a closing agent can get a check from the new lender, he or she must have the following:

- Final escrow instructions signed by the buyer and seller

- Signed loan documents

- Certified check or money order from the buyer

- Instructions from the buyer and seller to record the deeds on a certain date

The closing agent puts a cover letter—or "funding letter"—with the package and sends it to the lender's closing department for review. The cover letter details all the documents in the loan package. Now the closing agent for the lender goes through the package with a fine-tooth comb. Should an error be found, even as small as a missing initial, it must be corrected before the lender will release funds.

When everything is satisfactory with the loan package, the lender's closing agent contacts the escrow closing agent, gives the okay to record documents with the county, and then releases funds for closing. Because time is usually of the essence—most sellers want their money *now*—it is a good idea to find out how this paperwork will go back and forth between the lender and the closing agent.

Usually a courier is involved, but most companies only have one courier, and, as mentioned earlier, the end of the month can be a madhouse. If you find yourself pressed for time, you may want to confirm with your lender that this will not be a problem.

Canceling Escrow

Escrow can be terminated at any time on mutual agreement of the parties involved. For example, what if someone loses a job or gets a divorce or dies? For whatever reason, if both parties agree, the closing agent should be notified of the cancellation.

The closing agent will send a letter of cancellation to everyone involved, which states what is to happen to the money in escrow and who pays bills that may have been incurred. Some closing agents also charge a cancellation fee, and the seller may be liable for the real estate commission.

Usually, the buyer also is out the appraisal and credit report fees that were collected at loan application. If the buyers are going to buy another house, they may be able to use the same loan application to qualify for another home. If the buyers stay with the same loan program and loan amount, the lender only may require the appraisal for the new property to be underwritten. Then the loan would be ready to go to closing.

If the buyer and seller do not agree on cancellation, the closing agent cannot release funds unless the sales contract or the escrow instructions specifically authorize the release of funds in the event of default. In this case, the only remedy may be for the parties to sue for release of funds.

QUESTIONS TO ASK A CLOSING AGENT

- May I have a copy of your fee schedule?

- Do you have a title department?

- What is your turnaround time after receiving documents from the lender?

- After signing papers, when does funding take place?

- What are your office hours?

- Will you provide me with a HUD 1 Settlement Statement to review at least 24 hours before closing?

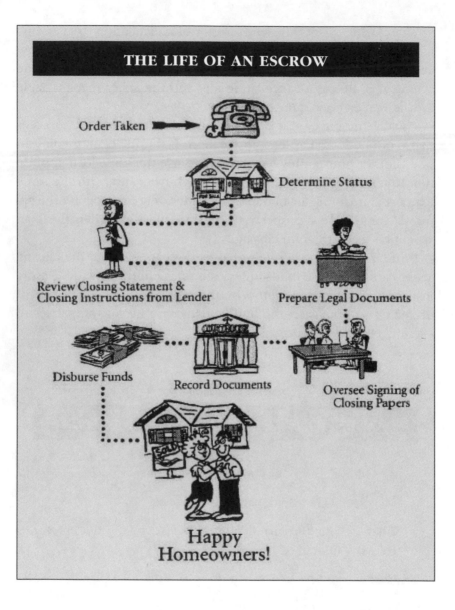

BEHIND THE SCENES FROM LOAN APPLICATION TO CLOSING

Now that you have put your real estate team in place, are you ready to make a loan application? Okay, here goes . . .

Step 1: Loan Origination

The buyer meets with a *loan officer,* possibly one referred by the real estate agent, to complete a loan application. The loan officer takes down all the information needed for the underwriter to determine the risk in making the loan. The property gets underwritten as well as the borrower.

The buyer usually is expected to pay an up-front fee for an appraisal and credit report at this time. The fee should be about $500, but be sure to ask how much is required in your geographic area.

The appraisal helps the lender to ensure it is not lending more than the property is worth. The appraiser is paid to protect the buyer and the lender. If the appraisal is inflated, then the buyer is at risk of overpaying for the property. Appraisers are limited in adding in value for amenities (examples might include upgraded carpet, wallpaper, quality fixtures, additional concrete walks and drives, or an oversized garage) that might have added value to the buyer but does not affect the market value.

Depending on your area, the typical turnaround time for an appraisal can be from two days to two weeks. FHA and VA loans sometimes take longer to close because homes closed on these loans cannot be appraised "as is." Work orders have to be written for repairs and the repairs completed before closing.

FHA now also requires a *Notice to the Homebuyer* form to be completed by the appraiser and submitted to the buyer at least five days prior to loan closing. The buyer also is to be given a *For Your Protection: Get a Home Inspection* disclosure to be signed before signing a contract with a seller. These forms are intended to protect the consumer by stressing the importance of home inspections and the condition of the property. Unfortunately, they have also added to the time and the cost of obtaining an FHA appraisal.

The credit report can take a few days to a few weeks, depending on the market and the lender. Credit reports and credit scores will be discussed in detail in Chapter 3. After the buyer signs all the required documentation, the loan officer turns the loan package over to a processor.

Step 2: Processing

The processor is responsible for setting up the file unless the lender has what is called a "setup person." Setting up a file means ordering a title report, credit report, and appraisal; setting up escrow settlement procedures; and typing up and mailing out verifications.

Verifications include verification of employment (VOE), verification of deposit (VOD), verification of rental or mortgage (VOR/M), and anything else that may be needed to help the underwriter determine the risk in making the loan.

The biggest problem with verifications is getting the people on the receiving end to fill them out and send them back. Most processors have a reminder system that lets them know when verifications should be returned and to follow up if they are not.

If this step gets left out, closing can be delayed because of something dumb like a landlord or apartment manager not sending back a VOR. Sometimes a buyer can get an employer or a past landlord to send in a verification when a processor is ignored.

Some of the things that can cause problems are VOEs with less time on the job than stated on the application, or income much lower, or "probability of continued employment" marked "Not Good." Another common roadblock is when a VOD has correction fluid used on it or amounts have been changed but not initialed by the bank employee filling out the verification.

Anything that does not match up or make sense has to be re-verified and that can be time consuming. If the processor gets too busy and forgets to look over a verification or the credit report, etc., and just puts it in the file, you could have big problems! Guess when you find out about it? After the file goes to the underwriter and gets turned down!

A good loan officer will review your files with the processor at least once a week. This way he or she can update the real estate agents involved, who can then update the buyer and seller.

It usually takes at least a week for anything to start coming back in on the file. It is the processor's responsibility to check every-thing as it comes in and make sure it matches up to the information given at loan application.

Processing can take from two to six weeks or more, depending on the current market conditions. In a "hot market" or when in-terest rates are low and a lot of people are refinancing, the turn-around time can slow down considerably.

Most lenders give priority to customers that they receive repeat business from. This is another reason a good team is critical to your success with real estate. If the loan does not close within the lock-in period, you may have to close at a higher rate or pay more to close at the rate you had originally locked in.

Time-Saver Processing Known as "Alt. Doc."

To speed up loan approval, buyers can use the time-saver pro-cessing method using alternative documentation (Alt. Doc.). The benefits of using this process include quicker closings and less stress on the buyer and seller. Instead of having to wait for verifi-cations to come back in, the buyer can bring the following to loan application:

Fast-Track Processing Checklist

VOE Verification of Employment	VOD Verification of Deposit	VOR/VOM Verification of Rental or Mortgage
Salaried: Last 2 years' W2s & most recent paycheck stub	Last 3 months' bank statements. Copies of CDs, stocks, bonds, etc.	Last 12 months' canceled checks (copied front/back)
Self-Employed/ Commissioned: 2 years' tax returns, Profit & Loss statement, balance sheet		or Year-end mortgage statement and recent canceled checks

Alternative documentation was started because of fraud. The lender would send out VOEs to companies, the applicant would intercept it in the mailroom, give it to his buddy, his buddy would fill out the form by inserting the income the applicant needed to qualify, sign it, and send it in to the lender. The result was that the lender would happily close the loan to someone who was not qualified and would often end up with a foreclosure.

The lenders smartened up and decided they needed to check the information on the VOE. The way they did this was to look at the W2 and most recent paycheck stub. Finally, some wise mortgage person somewhere said "Duh, why do we need the VOE at all, just get the stuff up front that we need to verify income." You see, there is hope! Alternative documentation was born out of that thought process. With the advent of underwriting software, the number of Alt. Doc. items needed even can be reduced and loans can be approved and closed a lot faster.

Okay, with standard processing, three or four weeks may have gone by and everything is back in on your file. The processor makes three separate copy packages of the entire file and can now submit the loan to *underwriting*.

Step 3: Underwriting

If the loan is a conventional loan with less than a 20 percent down payment, it may need to be submitted to two underwriters. One is the lender's underwriter and the other is what is called a private mortgage insurance (PMI) underwriter (see Chapter 4 for details about PMI). Some lenders have *delegated MI*. This means they have the authority to commit the mortgage insurance company themselves. This saves time and eliminates the need (and risk) of having another individual give an opinion of the risk involved in making the loan. The good news is that the underwriting process also is becoming streamlined with the advent of Fannie Mae's Desktop Underwriting and Freddie Mac's Loan Prospector underwriting software programs. In the past, lenders submitted credit files directly to FHA, VA, or a conventional investor. Conventional loans could take as much as two weeks in underwriting and FHA and VA even longer.

Aggressive lenders would go to visit the underwriter and beg them to get the file done and please approve it. Needless to say, the system got bogged down and a general transition was made. The lenders had to underwrite the loan according to the investor's guidelines and take some of the risk.

Lenders had to provide "reps" and warrants to the investors. That is, they had to represent and warrant to Fannie Mae, for instance, that the loan was underwritten according to its underwriting guidelines. The lender underwrites the loan, approves it, and sells it to Fannie Mae and everyone is happy and the consumer received better and faster service. Problems then arose due to Fannie Mae (and other investors) doing an audit and not agreeing that the loan was underwritten according to its guidelines!

The lender has agreed to buy any loan back that the investor tells them does not meet its guidelines. Well, the lender does not want to buy the loan back and it starts trying to talk its way out of buying back the loan. Do you see the problems this can create?

After a while, the industry discovered that the same types of loans tended to go into foreclosure. Several companies developed formulas for predicting which loans would not perform well. These formulas are called credit scores and will be discussed in detail in Chapter 3.

Credit scores enabled underwriting software to be developed that allows automatic underwriting. The borrower's information is entered into the computer, a credit report is pulled, and an underwriting recommendation is granted immediately! There are several decision levels that may be given, such as:

- *Approve/Eligible.* Based on data submitted, the loan meets eligibility requirements.

- *Approve/Ineligible.* The loan does not meet eligibility requirements based on product (type of loan) or LTV (loan-to-value), but does meet credit risk requirements. The loan must now go to an underwriter to see if there are additional circumstances to be considered.

- *Refer/Eligible.* The loan meets requirements but the risk factor should be reviewed by an underwriter.

- *Refer/Ineligible.* The loan does not meet eligibility requirements and an underwriter should review the loan.

- *Refer/Caution.* Due to a combination of risk factors, the loan does not appear to meet requirements. The credit risk is statistically greater than loans that receive a "refer" recommendation. This recommendation is not used for government loans (FHA or VA).

- *Out of Scope.* The software does not contain the rules needed to underwrite the product or borrower and results may not be valid.

One of the strengths of automatic underwriting is that lenders typically make loans to people who fit into all underwriting categories just fine, but if they miss just one paycheck, their house payment is at risk.

Based on the same set of guidelines, the person who just changed professions, although she has perfect credit and $200,000 in the bank, is rejected. The reality of automatic underwriting is that lenders now are able to make loans to people in that situation who might have a debt ratio of 50 percent but have perfect credit, plenty of money, and a history of handling similar debt load.

Once the loan has been submitted to underwriting that means you can go to closing tomorrow, right? Wrong! Most lenders have a 48-hour turnaround time in underwriting. There may be a whole stack of loans waiting for underwriting before yours gets there.

If something is missing or there is a problem, the loan can either get rejected or put into suspension until the problem is resolved. When it goes back to the underwriter it gets priority and gets looked at right away, right? Wrong!

It may go to the bottom of the stack or at least have to wait until the underwriter completes the file he or she is currently looking at. See why it is so important to get it right the first time? If your processor keeps asking for information after the application has been taken, do not get frustrated. The processor is just trying to give the underwriter as much information as possible that will help make the decision in your favor. Chapter 3 will give you more information on what the underwriter looks at to determine the risk in making the loan. Sometimes it is better to overdo it with information than to leave something out that could cause a delay.

At last, loan approval! Now we can close tomorrow, right? Wrong!

Step 4: Lender's Closing Department

Now the loan goes to the lender's closing department. The closing department draws up instructions for the closing agent (whoever is actually going to meet with the buyers and sellers and sign documents).

There may be a 48-hour turnaround time here, too. Remember, your loan is not the only loan the lender is working on.

Step 5: Closing Agent

Next a courier takes the loan package and closing instructions to the closing agent. You guessed it! There also may be a 48-hour turnaround time here. The buyer and seller meet with the closing agent to sign all the required documents and pay closing costs.

The papers then may have to be sent back to the lender's closing department to be reviewed before funds can be disbursed. If everything looks good, the lender releases funds and the loan is considered closed. This can sometimes be a day or two after signing. Make sure instructions for taking possession of the property and prorating of interest, taxes, and insurance are clearly spelled out in the purchase and sales agreement.

Some lenders actually will predraw documents. This means that the legal papers already are prepared when the loan is approved. The approval is matched with the documents and then released to the closing agent. This saves time and makes the process go smoother.

Some lenders also can table fund your transaction. That simply means they give the closing agent the authority to disburse funds prior to the lender seeing the closing papers. Lenders put themselves at risk when they do this, but if a lender is going to provide the utmost in customer service, then this is a very real option. So, if it's legal in your state, you should seek out a lender that offers table funding.

It could have taken anywhere from five to ten days from the time the loan was submitted to underwriting to the time the signing actually took place. Make sure you give yourself plenty of time for closing to take place when your write your contract.

Also keep in mind that technology is constantly improving and that procedures vary depending on your local market and on your lender. Once you select a lender to work with, have it review its turnaround times and procedures with you up front so you know what to expect.

BEHIND THE SCENES REVIEW

Step 1: Meet with the loan officer.

- Buyer brings information from a list of requirements.

- Loan officer completes paper work.

- Buyer pays up-front fee.

- Buyer selects lock option and loan officer writes lock-option agreement.
  - Lock free for 60 days?
  - Floating

- Average turnaround time: 1 to 2 hours

Step 2: Processor sets up the loan file.

- Orders the title report.

- Orders the credit report.

- Orders the appraisal.

- Sets up escrow.

- Sends out verifications: Verification of Employment (VOE), Verification of Deposit (VOD), Verification of Rental or Mortgage (VOR/M) (if Alt. Doc. is not used).

- Average turnaround time: (varies with lenders)

Verifications:	7 to 14 days
Appraisal:	5 to 10 days
Credit Report:	1 to 24 hours
Title Report:	2 days

(continued)

Step 3: Underwriter reviews the loan.

- Determines the risk.

- Requests PMI (private mortgage insurance) approval, when necessary.

- Approves/rejects the loan.

- Average turnaround time: 48 hours.

Step 4: Goes to lender's closing department.

- Prepares loan package for closing agent that will close the loan.

- Draws up closing instructions.

- Sends loan package to the closing agent.

- Average turnaround time: 48 hours.

Step 5: The loan closes.

The closing agent may work for the lender or may be a title company, escrow company, attorney, or in some cases, the real estate agent. The closing agent meets with the buyers and sellers.

- Has papers from the lender signed.

- Reviews closing instructions.

- Releases funds.

- Records documents.

- Average turnaround time: 48 Hours.

Note: The closing turnaround time is the approximate time the closing agent needs to complete the entire process. The time the buyer and seller actually meet with the closing agent is usually between 30 minutes to 1 hour.

SUMMARY

When you stop to consider how many people are involved before a transaction can close, it is a wonder it ever gets accomplished! Buying and selling real estate can be a very emotional time. That is why it is essential to your success with real estate to have a solution-oriented team standing by to handle any problems that may come up. Remember, the essence of a team is a common purpose or goal.

A good agent already will have taken the time to build a real estate service team that holds each other accountable for excellent service. If a problem does occur, the issue is not who caused the problem or why. The issue is how to solve the problem so the team can achieve its goal: a successful closing. No one wins if the loan does not close.

This means the loan officer, listing agent, selling agent, buyer, and seller may have to get involved if a problem occurs. If the loan officer knows the agents or the buyers or sellers are going to be accusatory instead of being useful, they may not be encouraged to disclose any potential problems until it is too late to resolve them. If there is a problem, you want it taken care of before the loan goes to the underwriter.

Give yourself plenty of time to complete processing and allow time to handle any problems that may come up. The sellers usually are ready to move to their new home and have to coordinate moving times; the buyers usually want to move in yesterday. Everyone is emotional enough without adding the stress of not having time to handle unexpected problems.

Although you may feel it is commonplace for lenders to drag their feet and waste your time, there are lenders who have made it their business to buck the trends and do things better. When picking your team, make sure your lender has a reputation for great service. Make sure it has an executive who is accessible, and an office and times where the lender can be seen. Lenders should be a part of the community and should look and act like a business. You do not have to accept bad service from any member of your team, because good service does exist. You can find it by taking the time to ask real estate professionals detailed questions up front and letting them know your goal is to build long-term relationships with your real estate team.

Statistics now show the average American moves every 3 to 5 years. Many also often invest in real estate, and I have one investor I work with that bought 15 houses this year. So long-term relationships really pay off in our business, and it benefits a consumer to build a real estate service he or she can work with long term instead of having to start over with each new purchase and sale.

BUYER'S CHECKLIST FOR LOAN APPLICATION

Mortgage information for: _____

❑ Current and previous addresses for a two-year period

❑ Social Security numbers

❑ Current and previous employers for at least two years for borrower and coborrower

❑ Complete addresses, account numbers, and current balances for all banks and credit unions

❑ Type and amount of other assets (stocks, bonds, life insurance, automobile values, and so on)

❑ Names of creditors, addresses, monthly payments, balances, and account numbers for all monthly obligations

❑ Income information for all wage earners

❑ Verification of other income, including retirement, pension, insurance, child support, and Social Security

❑ Copy of divorce decree, if applicable

❑ For VA and FHA/VA loans, copy of Veteran's DD214 or Certificate of Eligibility

❑ Copy of fully executed Earnest Money Agreement

❑ Information on real estate loans, currently owned property, or any property owned in the past two years

❑ Current, signed lease agreements for any real estate that is or will be leased

(continued)

❏ Copy of the pending contract if current home is to be sold

❏ Copy of all transfer benefits if a company transfer is involved

❏ All documents for bankruptcy or foreclosure and letter of explanation

To speed up loan approval, buyers can use the time-saver processing method (Alt. Doc.). The benefits of using this process include quicker closings and less stress on the buyer and seller.

Alternative Documentation

VOE	VOD	VOM/R

Salaried:
  Last 2 years'
  W2s & most
  recent pay-
  check stub
	Last 3 months'
	bank statements.
	Copies of CDs,
	stocks, bonds, etc.
		Last 12 months'
		canceled checks
		(copies front/back)
		
		or

Self-Employed/
Commissioned:
  2 years' tax
  returns, Profit &
  Loss statement,
  balance sheet
		Year-end mortgage
		statement and
		recent canceled
		checks

CHAPTER TWO

Avoiding Lender Rip-Offs!

Caveat emptor is Latin for "let the buyer beware." Webster's Dictionary defines it as *"The axiom (a self-evident or universally accepted truth) that one who buys something does so at one's own peril (exposure to the risk of harm or loss)."*

This warning is not intended to frighten, but rather to remind you that it is your responsibility to learn all you can about one of the most important, and maybe most expensive, endeavors you may ever participate in—homeownership. After reading this chapter you will be able to

- sift through real estate information that you are bombarded with through the media and numerous other sources and select what is useful to help you make educated decisions;

- understand the language of lenders and recognize when you are given vague or misleading answers;

- confidently compare interest rates and other fees charged by lenders to ensure you are choosing the option that is right for you; and

- avoid being ripped off by unethical lenders at closing.

Prior to the 1990s, caveat emptor was pretty much the attitude toward buyers of real estate. Since then agencies have been created and rules have been put in place to try to protect consumers, and this phrase is not in use anymore.

Unfortunately, it probably should be, only it should be used for all consumers. There are so many options and so much confusion about the home buying and selling process that it can be intimidating. It is also easy for you to be taken advantage of if you do not have the right people in place to guide you through the process.

The key to buying and selling real estate without getting ripped off in the process is to remember the responsibility is yours to become as informed as possible. You need to learn all you can *before* you buy or sell, not during the process, or some of your lessons will be learned the hard way. At your expense!

Some readers may be thinking, "That is easy for the author to say, but where do I start?" You have already taken the first step by reading this book. Fannie Mae also has some fantastic materials available to help educate consumers and all you have to do is call 800-7-FANNIE or visit its Web site at www.fanniemae.com.

There also are some very professional real estate agents, loan officers, and title companies who believe educating their customers is the best way to achieve successful closings. The Internet is also a continuing source of useful information. There is a lot of information available about buying and selling real estate. The key is to sift through the information and select what is useful to help you make educated decisions.

Some Things to Beware Of

Bait and Switch

Some unethical lenders use the old bait and switch routine. They will advertise or tell you on the phone that they have a certain loan program or interest rate available and then when you get there it is not available to you for one reason or another. They even may take your loan application (and your application fee) and wait a week or two before informing you of the change.

Or even worse, all along you were told you are getting a 7 percent interest rate and your total closing costs are $2,000. You are approved, no problem! You get to closing, you notice your rate is now 7.375 percent and your closing costs have gone up to $3,200. You think there is some kind of mistake so you call the same number and you get the same old voice mail from your loan officer. Except this time you don't get a call back. You are sitting in closing; your apartment has been leased; your furniture is sitting in a moving van; the seller is in the outer room; his furniture is sitting on the truck; the seller of the house he is buying is coming in to close in 30 minutes. . . . Get the picture?

You say, "Wait, I can't close. My rate is too high. My closing costs are all wrong . . . I do not know why my loan officer has not called me back, she has always been very responsive." Sound familiar? You have just been had by a system that in many states will allow a lender to do just what we have described. Did you think the deal was too good to be true? The unscrupulous lender just made more on you than any other legitimate lender you may have talked to when you were shopping around. You may be thinking, "No problem, I could just delay closing." But you can't.

The problem is that the seller could care less about your problems and he has a contract that says you are going to close. If you refuse, you are in breach of contract. And where are you going to stay tonight with your furniture? The lender has made a high percentage guess that you will be forced to close.

If you show up at a car dealer and you have ordered a red car and when you get there the dealer rolls out a green one, what do you do? You get in your old car until the dealer does what he has promised. It does not happen that way with real estate closings because the pressure to close comes from so many different sources. Unfortunately, the unethical lender is usually correct in assuming you will have to close. One way to avoid the "bait and switch" scam is to lock in your interest rate and ask for the lock-in agreement in writing.

Locking in the Interest Rate

When you make loan application you should be informed that you have an option to lock in your interest rate or let it "float" and lock it in sometime between loan application and a few days before closing.

You should ask the lender if it will give you a contract that guarantees the rate. Lenders should be willing to give you, in writing, the terms that go with a rate lock and be willing to stand behind it.

Most lenders lock in for 60 days for free but may charge a fee to lock in an interest rate for more than 60 days. Some lenders may not be willing to lock in the rate at loan application because they want to wait to lock until the loan is approved. There is not a problem with that as long as both the buyer and the seller understand the risk involved if rates should go up before the loan is locked in. If rates go up, the buyer may not be able to qualify for the loan unless someone pays discount points to buy the rate back down to the rate that was available at loan application.

You can choose an interest rate at "par," which means with zero discount points. One discount point equals 1 percent of the loan amount. On a $100,000 loan that equals $1,000 for every point that is required. Or you can choose to pay discount points and receive a lower rate. The discount points increase the yield to the lender, allowing you to have a lower interest rate on your loan.

Rates vary by lender and may change on a daily basis. They have even been known to change two or more times in one day.

SAMPLE QUOTE SHEET					
FHA		**VA**		**Conventional**	
7.5%	3 + 1	7.5%	3.25 + 1	7.5%	3.25 + 1
8%	0 + 1	8%	0 + 1	8%	0 + 1

In the preceding quote sheet, an FHA loan at 7.5% has three discount points. On a $100,000 loan that would equal $3,000. The interest rate with par pricing, or zero discount points, is at 8 percent. You can choose to pay discount points and receive a lower rate or choose a higher rate to avoid paying points at closing. There is also an origination fee that varies by lender. One origination fee equals 1 percent of the loan amount. In the sample quote sheet, the origination fee is quoted as + 1.

When you ask some lenders for a quote, they will give you the interest rate and the points, "7.5% with three points." Others will give you the interest rate and then combine points and the origination fee and simply say, "7.5% is at four points."

At first glance that does not seem to be a problem. It could be, though, if you assume both quotes include the origination fee. What if "7.5% with three points," also has a 2 percent origination fee? Always clarify how the rates and points are being quoted by asking, "Does that include the discount points and the origination fee?"

Lenders can offer lower discount points with shorter lock in periods. It could take you 30 to 60 days for loan approval in your market. You may think one lender sounds competitive and then find out when you make loan application that the quote you were given on the phone was for a 10-day lock and the other lenders were quoting you 60-day lock pricing.

Should you choose a lender based on price? Unless you are going to lock in your loan at loan application, it probably does not matter who has the lowest price the day you shop rates. Typically one lender may have the lowest rate one day and another may have the lowest the next day. You also have the most leverage with the lender *before* you make loan application, not *after.*

Once you have paid for your appraisal and credit report and completed the loan application, how likely are you to shop rates? If you float the loan and lock in a few days before closing, how do you know if you are getting the best rate the lender has available? Do you see that integrity of the loan officer is really more important than price?

You should not always believe what you read in the paper either. Quotes in the paper are at least three days old and are not guaranteed. Many lenders put below-market quotes in the paper to get you to call. All lenders basically go to the same markets and the same sources for money. Within a narrow range, all mortgage money should be the same. If a reputable lender gives you a quote and then you get another quote that seems too good to be true, beware! It probably is. The old bait and switch is alive and well in mortgage quoting!

Loan Officers Who "Play the Market"

The other danger to be aware of about interest rates is loan officers who "play the market." Playing the market means they think rates are going to go down and they want to wait until rates go below what they told the buyer at loan application so they can lock it in at the lower rate and make a higher commission on the loan.

Take Peter and Susan Morales, for example. They were buying their first home. They had applied for a loan and were told, "Everything looks good." Their loan officer told them their rate was locked in and they should close in 60 days.

They were so excited, they told all of their family and friends, gave notice at their apartment and took time off work to pack. Two days before closing they received a phone call from the processor telling them their loan had been rejected. Rates had gone up from the time they made loan application to the time they were supposed to close.

A closer look into the file revealed that the loan officer had never locked in their loan. He was waiting for rates to go down. When they started going up he kept thinking that they would surely come down again before it was time to close. He panicked but did nothing. By the time the loan was ready to close, the rates had gone up so much Peter and Susan could not qualify for the payment and did not have the money to buy the rate down.

Unfortunately, this is a common practice among a lot of loan officers. It is a dangerous game to play, especially for inexperienced loan officers. They come into an office and see the "old pros" playing the market all the time. Many of these "old pros" like to brag about how much extra money they make because of their expertise in playing the market.

Because most loan officers are paid on commission, it can be hard for a new loan officer to resist the opportunity to take a chance to make more money. Many of them do not even realize it is a risk. If rates have been fairly stable or declining, they may feel confident that there really is not a risk involved. After all, everybody else does it!

A consumer can reduce the risk of this happening to her or him by asking questions up front and getting everything in writing—especially the lock-in agreement. Even if you decide to "float" and lock in closer to closing, the lock-in agreement should be offered at loan application. Most agreements have an area to be initialed showing you elected to float instead of locking in the rate.

Also, do not forget to ask the lender "What is your policy on overages?" Many loan officers take offense when consumers or agents ask that question. If you want to add a lender to your team or an agent refers a customer to a lender, it only makes sense to understand how the lender operates. And that includes its policy on overages.

An overage means the difference in the rate given to the borrower and the rate that is actually locked in by the lender. This subject is not brought up to indicate that overages should not be charged. The issue is that loan officers should not tell you that you are locked in and not actually lock in your rate and they should not abuse overages.

Loan officers who use and abuse overages (charging excessive amounts) are not going to feel comfortable discussing their policy. At the same time, loan officers who have placed a value on their time and expertise and have set a policy for overages, should not have a problem telling customers how much they charge.

Some companies have a policy that a maximum of one point (1 percent of the loan amount) can be charged as an overage. Not all lenders have a policy in place. That means their loan officers decide how much to charge with each customer.

Lenders set pricing daily and it is up to loan officers to set their fees. They do this based on a number of things, one of which is competition and what the market will bear. It is fair to place a value for their time. If they cannot meet their income goals and pay bills, they cannot stay in the business.

Therefore, they carefully should estimate the hours they work, the average time spent with each loan applicant from loan application to closing, and determine what they need to make from each loan to make it worth their time and effort.

They should not have a problem with telling customers what they charge up front. Customers who do not feel the services are worth the fee should have the opportunity to go elsewhere.

Would you go to an attorney or a doctor without asking about fees up front? When an agent takes a listing, he or she negotiates the listing commission and then puts it in writing. Why should it be any different for a loan officer?

Junk Fees versus Administration Fees

In addition to discount points and origination fees, you will pay fees at closing that are sometimes called "standard closing costs and prepaids." Standard closing costs include appraisal fees, title insurance fees, discount points, origination fees, recording fees, escrow fees, credit report fees, flood certification, and tax service fees.

Prepaids include property taxes, insurance, and prorated interest that is collected to set up your escrow or reserve account with your lender.

Then there are fees that are commonly known as "junk fees." Items often called junk fees include:

- Document preparation fees

- Underwriting fees

- Processing fees

- Warehousing fees

- Application fees

Some could argue that you cannot originate a loan without underwriting it, processing it, etc. The lenders already are charging an origination fee, so extra fees charged for these services are junk fees, right?

Not necessarily. The cost of originating loans has steadily grown. It has been estimated that it costs approximately $2,500 to originate one loan. To cope with these costs, lenders have had to add certain fees to the closing costs in addition to standard fees charged. This has caused a lot of controversy and confusion over what is a fair administration fee and what is a junk fee.

Back in the 1970s, rates were generally quoted at the true rate. The true rate was the rate in terms of the cost of the money over 30 years or 15 years. As rates became more and more competitive, with consumers shopping rates, the market place drove rates down. The lending industry then came up with the extra fees that are now called "junk fees" or "administration fees," depending on your point of view. Lenders charge these fees to get their gross profit where it needs to be for them to stay in business. These fees should range from $500 to $800.

So how can you tell the difference between junk fees and administration fees? The best way is to ask three or more lenders to prepare a good faith estimate of charges for you on the loan amount you want.

SAMPLE GOOD FAITH ESTIMATE

Applicants: Joe & Mary Buyer   Date: 1/00

Type of Loan: Conventional   Term: 30 Year   Rate: 9%

Sales Price: $100,000   Loan Amount: $95,000   LTV: 95%

(continued)

Estimated Monthly Payment		Prepaids & Reserves	
Principal & interest	$764	Property taxes (4 months)	$500
Taxes	125	Insurance (14 months)	560
Hazard insurance	40	Homeowners dues	----
Mortgage insurance	60	30 days' interest	703
Homeowners dues	----	Total prepaids/	
Total house payment	$989	reserves	$1,763

Estimated Closing Costs

Origination fee (1%)	950		
Discount fee (0%)	----	**Summary**	
Title insurance	200	Down payment	$5,000
Appraisal fee	350	Total closing costs	2,370
Credit report	80	Total prepaids/reserves	1,763
Recording fee	20	**Estimated Cash**	
Escrow fee	325	**to Close**	$9,133
Document preparation*	195		
Tax registration	65	(Lender also may want to	
Underwriting fee*	185	verify that you will have	
Appraisal review	----	two to three total house pay-	
Other	----	ments left in your bank account	
Total Estimated		after closing.)	
Costs**	**$2,370**		

*These items, sometimes referred to as "junk fees," should be compared with two or three lenders to get a feel for what is reasonable.

**This is an estimate only. It may not cover all of the items you will be required to pay—in cash—at closing.

Annual Percentage Rate (APR)

Also ask the lender to give you the annual percentage rate (APR). The APR is the interest rate and the closing costs paid the first year. Lenders charging higher fees will be identified with higher APRs.

Many times buyers just look at interest rates and discount points when determining which lender to go to. However, anyone who has been in real estate any length of time will tell you that integrity is more important than price.

After all, anyone can promise you great rates, it is another thing to deliver quality service and actually get the loan closed as promised! If price is an issue and you decide to shop around, be sure to look also at the APR.

The APR will give you a more accurate picture of the actual cost of obtaining the loan. In real estate, the APR generally means the relationship of the principal and interest payment to the net proceeds of a loan: the stated loan amount less nonrecurring points and/or fees paid at origination.

❗ BEWARE

● In many states lenders do not have to give you the deal they quoted you. The Real Estate Settlement Procedures Act (RESPA) requires lenders to give you a good faith estimate of closing costs, but it does not require them to honor it. It is just an estimate. It is up to you to compare the original estimate to the settlement statement (also known as the HUD 1) you are given at closing. Always try to review it before going to closing so you have time to hold the lender to the original quote. If you are working with a good lender and real estate agent, they should review the HUD 1 before you even see it. If there are mistakes, they should correct them before you even have to be aware of it. This is another good reason to schedule your closing before the last week of the month so your agent has time to review the paperwork before you go to closing.

Lenders also charge fees to the seller of the property if the loan is an FHA or VA loan. In most states there is no requirement that the lender disclose these fees to the seller. If you are the buyer and your poor sellers are hit with $1,500 in fees they were not expecting, it could literally cost you the closing. How can that happen, you ask?

What if the sellers have no equity in the home and no cash to bring to closing? What if the sellers have cold feet anyway and this gives them an excuse to blow off the deal? Let the lender know up front that if the HUD 1 does not match the original good faith estimate (within reason) that you are not going to close. Also request that the seller be given a disclosure well in advance of closing of fees they may be expected to pay.

Compare the fees charged, especially those in the junk fee category. If a lender is charging excessive amounts in these areas compared to other lenders, it is time to ask questions and let it know you are comparing with other lenders. Sometimes a lender may be willing to match the fees in this area that other lenders are charging, and may even be willing to eliminate some of them. As the old saying goes, you never know until you ask! The trick is to know what to ask.

On FHA and VA government loans, the junk fees cannot be charged to the buyer. As mentioned earlier, if the lender is going to charge them to the seller, the seller should be informed that they will be included so he or she does not get to closing and then get upset because they are receiving less at closing than what their real estate agent had estimated.

One of the common complaints buyers and sellers have about the real estate process is that it always costs more than what they were originally told.

What seems to be the most upsetting is that they are not informed about it until they get to closing. This causes hard feelings because they feel like they are being manipulated. Good communication between you and your team is critical to the success of the team.

Builders' Mortgage Companies

A common practice of builders who own mortgage companies is as follows: You go into your friendly builder; let us say the builders name is Big John's Homes. You buy the home and the salesperson asks when you want to set up your loan application with Big John's Mortgage Company?

You thank them for the offer and tell them you are already preapproved with another lender. The salesperson says that is fine but that the builder will not pay for your title policy or for some other cost and/or upgrade. In the case of the title policy that can run, in some states, around $1,200 on a $100,000 home. Your mind immediately assumes you are talking about the same deal and the only difference is that the builder's deal is going to be $1,200 better. This is not always true. You need to compare rates and fees.

Another factor is that the home is probably to be built and you will not even lock in your rate until many months down the road. At that time you have your loan application in with Big John's Mortgage and that gives them leverage. The day comes to lock in your rate and the salesperson is happy to inform you that your rate at Big John's has been locked in at 7.25 percent and they can close you any time.

The problem is that current rates are not 7.25 percent, they are actually 6.75 percent and you have just been taken for $2,000. The builder now has an additional $2,000 available profit to pay for the $1,200 title policy and a handsome $800 profit to boot. Builder-owned mortgage companies can be a huge profit center for them, although many builders own their own mortgage companies so they can deliver what they believe to be better service and to protect themselves from unscrupulous lenders. Remember to get everything in writing.

RESPA

The *Real Estate Settlement Procedures Act (RESPA)* is one of the most important acts that has been put into place to protect consumers:

> *RESPA encourages home ownership by regulating certain lending practices, and closing and settlement procedures in federally related mortgage transactions to minimize costs and difficulties of home purchase.* *

Barron's Real Estate Handbook by Jack C. Harris, Ph.D., and Jack P. Freidman, Ph.D., CPA, MAI, Barron's Educational Series. 1993. pg. 77.

RESPA was created in 1974, amended in 1975, and is continually under scrutiny by the government, the National Association of REALTORS® (NAR) and the Mortgage Bankers Association (MBA). The idea behind RESPA is that it will protect consumers from being taken advantage of in the home buying process. The only problem is that not all agents or lenders abide by its guidelines.

If you are not educated in the steps involved in buying and selling real estate, you do not even know if someone is taking advantage of you.

One of RESPA's guidelines states that the lender is required to make a Truth-in-Lending disclosure and give the buyer a good faith estimate within three days after loan application.

These disclosures are usually mailed to the buyer and include the following:

- Itemized costs incurred with the loan

- The interest rate charged

- Whether the lender will be transferring the servicing rights on the loan

- If the loan is an adjustable-rate mortgage (ARM), a "worst case scenario" must be disclosed showing how high the payments and interest could possibly rise.

It would make more sense if these disclosures were required to be made in person, at the time of loan application. Most consumers get this information in the mail and simply sign it and mail it back to the lender without even reading it. Or they do read it but it does not make any sense and they do not want to ask questions and admit they do not understand it. After all, they do not want to do anything that would jeopardize getting loan approval.

The Truth-in-Lending disclosure, better known as the TIL, can be especially confusing. The purpose of the TIL is to disclose to the consumer the terms and costs of obtaining the loan.

The lender must disclose to the buyer the APR, which we mentioned earlier and is the interest rate and closing costs paid on the loan expressed as a yearly rate, the finance charge, the amount financed, and total of payments.

However, this can be very confusing for most buyers. When they see the APR on the TIL, it reflects a rate higher than the interest rate they were told at loan application. That is because it reflects the additional fees being charged at closing. A sample TIL can be found on page 65.

The explanation for TIL terms usually is provided on a separate sheet of paper for the consumers to make of it what they will. For example, the explanation for the APR being different from the note rate reads as follows:

Annual Percentage Rate

This is not the Note rate for which the borrower applied. The Annual Percentage Rate (APR) is the cost of the loan in percentage terms taking into account various loan charges of which interest is only one such charge. Other charges, which are used in calculation of the Annual Percentage Rate, are Private Mortgage Insurance or FHA Mortgage Insurance premium (where applicable) and Prepaid Finance Charges (loan discount, origination fees, prepaid interest, and other credit costs).

The APR is calculated by spreading these charges over the life of the loan, which results in a rate higher (or lower) than the interest rate shown on your Mortgage/Deed of Trust Note.

If interest were the only finance charge, then the interest rate and the annual percentage rate would be the same. Then the buyer sees finance charge, which is the dollar amount the credit will cost the buyer. This amount can be almost twice as much as the loan amount applied for. It is explained as:

Finance Charge

The amount of interest, prepaid finance charges, and certain insurance premiums (if any) that the borrower will be expected to pay over the life of the loan.

Next comes amount financed and it is less than the loan amount they need to buy the home. That is because lenders are required to show the amount financed as the loan amount less prepaid finance charges paid at closing. It is explained as:

Amount Financed

The Amount Financed is the loan amount applied for, less the prepaid finance charges. Prepaid finance charges can be found on the Good Faith Estimate. For example, if the borrower's note is for $100,000 and the prepaid finance charges total $5,000, the amount financed would be $95,000.

The Amount Financed is the figure on which the annual percentage rate is based.

Then the total of payments, which is the amount paid after all total house payments have been made, is listed and this is approximately three times the amount borrowed. Talk about intimidating!

The point is, most consumers would benefit from having a real estate professional read through this information and answer any questions they may have.

Price versus Integrity

By now you should be realizing that the most important thing you can do when choosing a real estate agent and a lender is to look for integrity, not just price. You can be promised the best price up front, but end up with something entirely different at closing.

It is a good idea to ask for references of past customers and ask other people in the real estate field about the person you are thinking about working with. Take Ellen and Ross Watson, for example.

Ellen and Ross Watson were told at loan application that they would be charged one discount point. When they got to closing, they were being charged a point and a half. When the closing agent called the lender, the manager told them that the loan ended up

TRUTH-IN-LENDING DISCLOSURE STATEMENT

Lender: ABC Mortgage Company
            One First Parkway
            Kalamazoo, MI 12345
Borrowers: John & Mary Daugherty
Address: 123 Anyplace
            Everywhere, TX 65432

Annual Percentage Rate	Finance Charge	Amount Financed	Total of Payments
Cost of your credit as a yearly rate.	The dollar amount the credit will cost.	The amount of your credit provided to you on your behalf.	The amount you will have paid after you have made all payments as scheduled.
8.298%	$170,908.89	$98,869.05	$269,777.94

PAYMENT SCHEDULE:

Number of Paymt's	Amount of Paymt's	Paymt's Due Mthly & Begin	Number of Paymt's	Amount of Paymt's	Paymt's Begin
359	749.39	11/1/99			
1	746.93	10/1/99			

taking "a lot of work." Because there was a point and a half in the contract that the seller could pay, they went ahead and charged it.

The loan was a typical loan; it closed in 30 days and was not any extra work that the buyers had been aware of. The sad thing about this is that the sellers had bought the home only one year ago and had taken out a second lien to put in a swimming pool.

They had relocated out of state and actually were having to pay $4,000 just to close the house! When that was pointed out to the lender, it said it did not make a difference because the contract said the seller was willing to pay "up to one and a half points" and that was what they were going to pay!

This is where a good real estate agent comes in. If the Watsons had used a lender referred by the agent, the end result might have been different. Most good real estate agents have taken the time to carefully put together a team to provide their customers with quality service.

Which of the following do you think will get the best service and rates from a lender?

- *Buyer A:* Referred to a lender by a real estate agent that sends them a lot of business.

- *Buyer B:* Buyer chose the lender out of the phone book.

Buyer A will most likely get preferential treatment because the lender knows that the real estate agent will be overseeing its customer's transaction and the lender will hope to get future business referred to them by the agent.

SUMMARY

Applying for a mortgage loan can be stressful whether you have perfect credit or the worse credit history on the planet. Try not to be in too big of a hurry to make a decision that involves thousands of your dollars. Ask questions and understand the answers. Never assume everyone will be looking out for your best interests! Take the time to ask for explanations from real estate agents and lenders or contact one of the professional organizations discussed in this chapter. The more you understand the loan process the less likely you are to encounter problems at closing.

CHAPTER THREE

Qualifying for a Mortgage

The information in this chapter is important to buyers and sellers alike. Understanding what it takes for a "ready and willing" buyer to become an "able" buyer can save both sellers and buyers a lot of time and money. When you understand how the lender looks at your income-to-debt ratios, and what it takes to get the best financing available, it makes you less vulnerable to those who would try to take advantage of you. After reading this chapter you should be able to

- use financing to help turn yourself from a "ready and willing" buyer into an "able" buyer.

- understand how the lender looks at your income and debt to determine your purchasing power (maximum loan amount the lender will allow).

- recognize the importance of your credit score and how to correct mistakes on your credit report.

Most buyers want to answer two questions:

1. What is the monthly payment?

2. How much will it cost me to close?

Once these two questions are answered, many ready and willing buyers are now able buyers. Sellers can have a lender prepare a Mortgage Comparison Sheet to give to buyers interested in your home to show them how your house can become their home. The Mortgage Comparison Sheet will show different loan options with different ratios, down payment, and closing costs requirements.

Buyers should talk to the real estate agent and loan officer on their team about prequalifications and preapprovals. An experienced agent can help determine purchasing power and prevent a lot of headaches.

A prequalification is based on verbal information you give your team. They can pull a preliminary credit report and discuss finding a loan that is right for you before you find your dream home.

Most lenders also are willing to do a preapproval. This means you actually apply for a loan and receive approval from the underwriter without having a property designated for the collateral.

When you do find your home, an appraisal is ordered and the underwriter then underwrites the property and issues you final approval for the loan.

Many times a preapproval gives you an advantage over other offers when you are negotiating with sellers. The more you understand about how the lender looks at your income, the easier it will be to make sure you find a loan you will be comfortable with.

THE FOUR CS OF UNDERWRITING

The lender's underwriter determines your purchasing power by using a set of guidelines to help determine the degree of risk in making the loan. The underwriter, whose job it is to look for the degree of risk, often uses the following Four Cs:

1. *Credit history.* How much do you owe; do you pay bills on time; how often do you borrow, do you live within your means; will you repay the loan?

2. *Capacity.* Income versus expenses; occupation, income, how long in same line of work; monthly debt obligations,

number of dependents, do you pay child support or alimony; can you repay the loan?

3. *Capital.* Is the money for down payment and closing costs coming out of your own funds or will you receive a gift from family members? How much money will you have left after closing?

4. *Collateral.* Is the value of the property sufficient to repay the loan in case of default? Will the lender be protected if you fail to repay the loan?

Credit History

Traditionally, underwriters used compensating factors to help offset the Four Cs. Now a new method called credit scoring is being used, and compensating factors do not carry as much weight as they use to.

What Is a Credit Score?

A credit score is a number that lenders use to predict the degree of risk in making a loan. The number is calculated using your past credit history. The credit score used most often by lenders is produced by a company called Fair Isaac & Company (FICO). Their scores range from 350 to 900; the lower the number, the greater the likelihood of default.

By evaluating the historical performance of loans with certain borrower credit characteristics, future performance of loans with similar credit characteristics can be predicted.

Factors that have the most influence on lowering credit scores are called reason codes. Four reason codes are given with each credit score. Examples include:

1. Too few accounts currently "paid as agreed"

2. Current delinquency (late payments)

3. Too many inquiries in the past 12 months

4. Proportion of balances to credit limits too high on trade lines (credit cards or open lines of credit)

Do Scores Change?

Most scores remain stable during short periods of time although any change in credit activity will result in a change to the score. It is possible for you to have scores pulled three different times and have a different score each time. The amazing thing about credit scores is that they will go down immediately but it takes a long time for them to go up. When your credit report is pulled, your score goes down. The thinking is that if someone is accessing your credit then you must be getting ready to buy something, therefore you are at greater risk of default.

❗ BEWARE

This means that if your score is borderline, in the low 600s, you could be prequalified based on your credit score and then have a different credit score if you wait to obtain approval until you find the right house. If the score is lower, the lender might charge you a higher interest rate.

A higher interest rate will result in higher monthly payments and also could affect the loan amount the lender will allow you. The best way to avoid this is to obtain a preapproval, as discussed in the previous chapter, as early as possible.

Credit scores are calculated using information from the nation's three largest credit reporting repositories. They are:

Trans Union	Equifax	Experian
(800) 916-8800	(800) 685-1111	(888) 397-3742
P.O. Box 390	P.O. Box 740256	P.O. Box 949
Springfield, PA	Atlanta, GA	Allen, TX
19064-0390	30374-0241	75013-0949

How Do Credit Scores Affect Underwriting a Loan?

Fannie Mae and Freddie Mac endorse the use of credit scores when underwriting loans. Underwriters are recommended to use the following approaches:

Credit Score	Approach Recommended
660 & above	Basic review
620–659	Comprehensive review
619 & below	Cautious review

Fannie Mae recommends that borrowers with low credit scores should have offsetting strengths as a means of compensating for the lower score. Compensating factors include the following:

- Strong equity position (large down payment)

- Debt ratios below the highest standard ratios

- Excess cash left in the bank after closing

- Successful history of paying housing expenses equal to the monthly housing expense requested if credit is given

Another challenge is for those rare people who have never used credit. You would think that the ability to stay on a cash basis would be good, however, a credit score of 0 is not advisable. If you do not use credit, you should consider starting with a credit card you pay off monthly as the bill comes in. That should give you a good score and, if you need a mortgage, lenders will be looking for one. At this time, the FHA and VA do not require credit scoring but that will probably change in the future.

Credit Scoring Benefits

- Can speed up loan approval for those with high scores.

- Generates more time to evaluate low scores.

- They are objective (the scoring model does not consider items such as race, sex, religion, or national origin).

- May help you avoid foreclosure if used correctly.

- They are predictive of mortgage default.

Credit Scoring Concerns

If the credit bureau makes an error, you have to correct it with the bureau and with FICO (the repository that provides scores).

❗BEWARE

The U.S. Public Interest Research Group (PIRG) is the national lobbying office for state PIRGs, a network of nonprofit consumer and environmental groups founded by Ralph Nader. They published a report called *Mistakes Do Happen*. The report states that nearly one-third of all consumer credit bureau reports contain serious errors that could cause denial of a mortgage, car loan, credit card, or even a job.

The group also reports the following:

- Each of the three national credit reporting companies processes more than two billion pieces of information from lenders each month.

- More than two million credit reports are issued each business day in the United States.

Consider the case of Robert Peter Smith, field director with Colorado PIRG:

Mr. Smith was told he could not be approved for a mortgage until he cleared up a $720 legal judgment filed against an R. Smith by Howard University Hospital in Washington, D.C.

The hospital bill turned out to be for a Renee Smith. The lender told Robert he still had to obtain a letter saying he was not liable for the debt.

He was told, "If it is owed, pay it, and if it is not you, you clear it up." Smith has stated, "After three weeks of camping out on the phone, I got the court to talk to the lender and straighten it out. But it was my burden to make this go away."

- *Creditors report to only one bureau.* This may cause problems if you have removed an item from your credit report with one bureau but it still shows up on others and is reported to FICO. You also may have good credit items that are not showing up on all bureaus.

- *Collectors/courts may not report to all bureaus.* Once paid, burden of cleaning up lies with individual.

- *Good credit may not mean a high score.* If you have numerous credit cards and open lines of credit, this will lower your score even if you pay them on time or even if they have no balances.

- *Spouses have different scores.* The lower of the two scores will be used. Sometimes credit items are the same but one score is lower than the other.

- *Duplicate reports.* The same credit item may show up more than once. This lowers the credit score because this affects lines of open credit and debt owed. Again, burden of cleaning up lies with individual.

- *Unethical lenders.* Consumers are not given their credit scores when they request their credit reports. The reason given for this is that they "have not been given the training to understand them and would be frustrated if they were told they could not receive a loan because their score was too low." Unfortunately, this attitude sets the consumer up to be taken advantage of by unethical lenders.

If you do not take the time to build a good team, credit scoring is an easy way for unethical lenders to take advantage of you. They may charge you a higher interest rate by telling you your credit score was too low to get a lower rate.

❗BEWARE

● Buyers with low credit scores due to late payments, bankruptcy, or past foreclosures often were rejected in the past. They were told they needed to clean up their credit and establish a good record for at least 24 months before they could obtain a loan.

Then a new market was established for buyers in this category. It is called subprime lending. Lenders realized they could make more money on these loans and many times these buyers were now a good risk.

There are some lenders who only offer subprime loans and do not understand or have outlets for standard loans. The subprime lender will offer the buyer an interest rate based on credit score. The lower the score, the higher the rate and closing cost. This is great for people who may have had credit problems but have been working to resolve them. They now can buy a home and establish a good credit history and possibly refinance at a lower rate in the future. The problem is that many people are being charged higher rates and fees than they really should have to pay. Take the O'Neils for example:

Peggy and Jack O'Neil were told at loan application that they were locked in at 7.5 percent on a $227,000 loan with no discount points. Five weeks later the loan officer called to tell them he had good news and bad news. The loan was ready to close but the interest rate was 10.4 percent because of their credit. On top of that, they were now going to have to pay three discount points ($6,810).

The O'Neils were in a position many people find themselves in if they have not put together a team that will look out for their best interests. If the O'Neils wanted to close on time on their home, they felt they had no choice but to close at the higher rate and fees. They also were embarrassed about their past credit problems and had not discussed the situation with their agent.

Luckily, this story has a happy ending. The O'Neils decided to talk to their agent about the problem before agreeing to close. The agent had another lender look at the loan. They found out that although the O'Neil's credit score was borderline, they had good compensating factors.

One of the compensating factors was that they had excess cash left over after closing. Could this be the reason the first lender wanted to charge three discount points? The second lender also looked at the good faith estimate and saw that the first lender was receiving a premium back from the investor it was brokering the subprime loan to.

The premium was approximately $1,800. The investor could have made the loan at 9.875 percent but the loan officer wanted to charge 10.4 percent and collect the premium on top of the origination fee and the three discount points.

The good news is that the O'Neils were able to transfer the loan to the second lender and ended up saving more than $7,000 in closing cost and $88.50 per month due to the lower interest rate.

One of the most important things you can do is find out immediately what your credit score is and then talk to your team about loan programs available to you with your score. Remember the credit score guidelines discussed earlier. If your score is higher than 620, you should be able to get the best pricing available. If it is lower than 620, there may be some things you and your team can do that will help raise your score. Keep in mind that lenders set their own benchmarks and some may require scores of 660 or better before offering standard rates.

You may want to contact the Consumer Information Center for free and low-cost federal publications of consumer interest. Their brochure titled "Ready, Set . . . Credit," shows you how to check your credit record and establish a good history. They also have a brochure titled "How to Dispute Credit Report Errors," that gives tips on correcting errors and registering a dispute. You can contact them on-line at http://www.pueblo.gsa.gov, or via phone at 714-948-4000 The Quicken Web site also provides valuable information on credit reports and resolving disputes. Their Internet address is www.quicken.com.

Capacity

The lender will look at your income to determine your capacity to repay the loan. In other words, your ability to repay the loan is based on your current income and debts. A good loan officer will present your loan where it gives the best perception to an underwriter. For example: A family with a single wage earner and five people in the family would not compare well with a family that has two wage earners who are the only ones in the family. The loan officer can write a cover letter to the underwriter pointing out the strengths of the file. In other words, a good loan officer will neutralize the negative aspects and emphasize the positive aspects of the loan.

One of the ways lenders determine capacity is by using debt-to-income ratios.

Calculating Ratios

A qualifying ratio is a percentage used by a lender to determine whether a buyer can qualify for a payment based on guidelines set by the secondary market. This percentage is determined by comparing debt to income.

A *front ratio* equals the *total house payment (THP)* divided by the *gross monthly income (GMI)*.

$$\text{Front Ratio} = \frac{\text{Total House Payment}}{\text{Gross Monthly Income}}$$

A *back ratio* also is used and it equals the *total house payment + debt* divided by the *gross monthly income.*

$$\text{Back Ratio} = \frac{\text{Total House Payment + Debt}}{\text{Gross Monthly Income}}$$

The THP includes principal, interest, taxes, hazard insurance, mortgage insurance, and homeowners dues, if applicable. Some people refer to the house payment as PITI. PITI is the principal, interest, taxes and insurance portion of your house payment. The debt is the minimum monthly payment required on credit cards; installment loans, such as, cars, boats, student loans, etc.; child support; and, on VA loans, child care.

Income and Expense Ratios for Loans

There are basically three types of standard loans with variations on those three. FHA and VA loans are referred to as government loans because they are backed by the government. Conventional loans are sold to the secondary market in which Fannie Mae is the largest purchaser.

Each type of loan has special guidelines and ratios the buyers must meet. We discuss the different loan options in the next chapter.

Ratios for each type of loan are as follows:		
*THP = Total house payment (PITI + MI and Homeowners Dues) *GMI = Gross monthly income *LTV = Loan-to-value (loan amount divided by value of the property)		
Conventional	**FHA**	**VA**
(varies with lenders)		
LTV > 90% 28/36	29/41	41%
LTV < 90% 33/38		Also check residual (explained below)

Example:

The buyer wants a THP of $1,000 per month. His debt equals $400 per month. What are his ratios and which loans allow those ratios?

Answer:

Remember to divide the THP by the gross monthly income and you will find the front ratio is 28.5 percent. Take the THP + debt and divide by the gross monthly income to find a back ratio of 40 percent. The buyer could qualify for an FHA loan because FHA ratios are 29/41. A buyer who is a veteran also could qualify for a VA loan because VA only uses one ratio of 41 percent. The back ratio of 40 percent is too high for a conventional loan.[1]

$$\frac{1,000}{3,500} = 28.5\% \text{ Front Ratio} \qquad \frac{1,000 + 400}{3,500} = 40\% \text{ Back Ratio}$$

Ratios versus Residual Income

Lenders use two guidelines to establish the maximum loan amounts for VA loans:

1. Income-to-debt ratio

2. VA residual income

As shown in the preceding chart, a veteran's total obligations to income ratio should not exceed 41 percent. Total obligations include Total House Payment (principal, interest, taxes, insurance and homeowners dues) + debts.

---

[1]These are guidelines only; some lenders may allow higher ratios.

Gross monthly income	$3,500
Maximum ratio	× .41
	$1,435
Monthly debts not including THP	− 500
Total House Payment (THP) allowed	$ 935

When determining a veteran's ability to repay a loan, the lender also looks at required minimum balances for family support as well as their 41 percent income-to-debt ratio. The amount required will vary by loan amount, region of country, and size of family. Your team lender can supply you with a chart with current amounts for your area.

These minimum balances are called *residual income* and are determined by looking at how much money is left over after the borrower pays all debt, including the new house payment. If the borrower's residual income exceeds the minimum required on the chart by 20 percent or more, a lender may approve a ratio higher than 41 percent.

The formula for calculating residual income is:	
Gross monthly income	$ _____
− Total house payment	− _____
− Monthly debts	− _____
− Withholding taxes	− _____
− Social Security	− _____
− Utilities and maintenance	− _____
= Residual income	$ _____

Capital

Your capital (down payment and closing costs requirements) will be based on the type of loan you choose. On VA loans you may be allowed to purchase a home with zero down payment and have the seller pay the closing costs. You also can have a gift from a family member to pay for closing costs or the down payment. FHA requires a minimum investment in the home, but it all can be a gift from a family member or close family friend.

Conventional loans require buyers to have a minimum investment in the home out of their own funds. Fannie Mae offers products, called Community Lending Products, which allow buyers in certain income limits or geographical locations to purchase a home with less money out of pocket than standard conventional loans.

As a rule of thumb you might expect the minimum capital needed for each type of standard loan to be as follows:

Type of Loan	Capital Needed
VA	Up to 3% of the loan
FHA	Up to 6% of the loan
Conventional	5% to 10% of the loan

Again, these are guidelines only. You may be required to pay less or possibly more than the above. There are also special loan programs available that may offer down payment assistance where you could purchase a home with no money out of pocket. You should contact your local lender to inquire about bond programs and other homebuyer assistance that may be available. Also, ask your loan officer to prepare a good faith estimate for you as discussed in Chapter 2.

Collateral

The *collateral* for your loan is your house. If you fail to make your payments on time, the lender can foreclose on your home. The lender determines the value of your collateral by the sales price or the appraisal, whichever is less.

Then, depending on which type of loan you choose, you must meet minimum loan-to-value ratio (LTV) requirements. The LTV is calculated by dividing the loan amount by the value of the home (sales price or appraised value).

For example, if the sales price is the value of the home:

$$\frac{\text{Loan Amount}}{\text{Sales Price}} = \text{LTV} = \frac{\$47,500}{\$50,000} = 95 \text{ percent LTV}$$

The LTV is used to determine your capital (down payment and closing costs) required for each type of loan. On a standard Fannie Mae conventional loan, the minimum LTV is 95 percent. (Community Lending Products allow lower LTVs.)

If your sales price is $100,000 and your LTV is 95 percent, you would need a down payment of 5 percent, which would be $5,000.

The Fifth C—Comfort Zone

The Four Cs help the lender determine the loan amount and monthly payment they will allow you. There is a Fifth C that is sometimes overlooked that is just as important, your comfort zone. Your comfort zone is how much of your income you are comfortable paying toward your house payment.

Even if you qualify for a higher monthly payment, you may not be happy in your new home if you are not comfortable with the monthly payment required. The Resources section at the end of this book has information for agencies that can help you create a spending plan that includes your responsibilities for your new home.

MORTGAGE WORKSHEET

The Mortgage Worksheet is a tool designed to make calculating the maximum loan amount for the buyer easier. If you have a real estate calculator you can complete this form yourself. Otherwise, you can review this form with your team so that you understand why you qualify for a certain loan amount. You will find a worksheet example on the next page. A blank worksheet has been provided for you at the end of this chapter.

To be referred to an agent or lender that can review this form with you and prequalify or preapprove you for a loan, check the Residential Financing Council (RFC) Web site at www.rfcouncil.com.

Mortgage Worksheet Example

The Mortgage Worksheet has been prepared for Joe and Mary Buyer. The lender will look at two ratios for FHA and conventional loans and one ratio for VA loans. After calculating the front and back ratios the lender will allow the buyer the lower of the two THPs. The total cash available, the credit score, the comfort zone, and the THP will help the lender determine which type of loans may be best for the buyer. After selecting the THP from the type of

MORTGAGE WORKSHEET EXAMPLE

Name: Joe & Mary Buyer   Phone Number: 555-1234

Comfort Zone: $1,000   Current Payment: $850

Down Payment: Minimum Allowed   Total Cash Available: $10,000

Credit History: Good   Credit Score: Unknown

Gross Monthly Income		How Long	Monthly Debts		Balance
Borrower:	$2,500	2 years	MC	$ 40	$1,400
Coborrower:	$1,000	3 years	Car	200	8,000
Bonus/Comm.:	———		Visa	30	935
Gross Income:	$3,500		Total:	$270	

Conventional (Ratios vary with lenders. Check with your team)

Gross Income $3,500 × Front Ratio 28% = THP $980

Gross Income $3,500 × Back Ratio 36% = $1,260 – Debts $270 = THP $990

FHA (Ratios are the same with all lenders)

Gross Income $3,500 × Front Ratio 29% = THP $1,015

Gross Income $3,500 × Back Ratio   41% = $1,435 – Debts $270 = THP $1,165

VA (Ratios same with all lenders. Also check residual with your team.)

Gross Income $3,500 × 41% = $1,435 – Debts $270 = THP $1,165

THP	$980	Interest Rate	9%	7%
– Taxes	125	Loan Amount	$94,000	$106,400
– Insurance	40	+ Down Payment	5,000	5,600
– PMI, MIP	60	Sales Price	99,000	112,000
P&I	$755	Closing Costs	$ 4,133	$ 4,133

loan selected, you then can fill in the box at the bottom of the work-sheet to determine the maximum loan amount the lender will allow.

SUMMARY

If homes that are on the market have a Mortgage Comparison Sheet available, buyers can look at different financing options that will help them purchase the home. Financing options should show the buyers different down payments required and different monthly payments so that buyers who thought they could not afford the home will see that there may be options that can work for their situation.

A good real estate team will educate buyers and sellers on the steps involved in buying and selling real estate in their market. The buyers should understand *why* they qualify for the loan amount the lender will allow.

Sellers and buyers also can benefit from understanding how the Four Cs affect their real estate transaction. The Four Cs as discussed earlier, include:

1. Credit history (past record of repaying debt)

2. Capacity (ability to make payments based on current income and debts)

3. Capital (down payment and closing costs required)

4. Collateral (value of the property being financed)

The Fifth C is your comfort zone. Your comfort zone is how much of your income you are comfortable dedicating toward your house payment. Some people will find they qualify for more than they are comfortable paying, while others may find they are comfortable with higher payments than the lender will allow.

Credit scores can be obtained by having the loan officer on your team pull a preliminary credit report. Buyers should consider obtaining loan preapproval as early in the homebuying process as possible because the credit score will determine the interest rate and loan program lenders will offer.

MORTGAGE WORKSHEET

Name: _____ Phone Number: _____

Comfort Zone: _____ Current Payment: _____

Down Payment: _____ Total Cash Available: _____

Credit History: _____ Credit Score: _____

Gross Monthly Income	How Long	Monthly Debts	Balance
Borrower			
Coborrower			
Bonus/Comm.			
Rental			
Total			

Conventional (Ratios: 95% LTV = 28/36, 90% and Below = 28/26)

Gross Income _____ × Front Ratio ___ % = THP* _____

Gross Income _____ × Back Ratio ___ % – Debts _____ = THP* _____

FHA

Gross Income _____ × Front Ratio ___ % = THP* _____

Gross Income _____ × Back Ratio ___ % – Debts _____ = THP* _____

VA

Gross Income _____ × Back Ratio ___ % – Debts _____ = THP* _____

(continued)

Total House Payment		Interest Rate		
– Taxes		Loan Amount		
– Insurance		+ Down Payment		
– PMI, MIP, H.O.		Sales Price		
Principal & Interest		Approx. Closing Costs		

Lenders usually require verification of one to three months total house payments (reserves) after closing costs and down payments.

The forms included in this packet are intended for the buyers' information only and intended solely for illustration purposes. The preparer assumes no liability nor guarantees the accuracy of the illustration. The buyers should seek competent tax and financial advice.

Chapter Four

Loan Options

The purpose of this chapter is to give buyers and sellers an overview of available financing options that will help you buy or sell a home. Being familiar with the options that are available will enable you to save thousands of dollars on your mortgage. After reading this chapter, sellers will be able to

- consider financing options before reducing your sales price.
- use financing strategies that will give your home the edge over the competition instead of just listing it at the lowest possible price.

After reading this chapter, buyers will be able to

- select loan options that will allow you to increase your purchasing power.
- purchase a home with less cash out of your pocket.

The more familiar buyers and sellers are with available loan programs, the more likely they are to save time and money when buying and selling real estate. Sellers should talk with a real estate professional and try to profile the types of buyers that might be interested in their home (first time buyers, move up buyers, empty nesters, etc.).

Many people spend weeks—even months—shopping for the right house and negotiating the best price. At the same time, sellers try to hold out for the highest price possible for their home. But, if you are not educated about loan options that are available to you, there is a good chance you could end up losing all the money you have tried to save and then some!

Knowledgeable real estate agents and loan officers will take the time to learn about a seller's and a buyer's needs. Then they will take the time to educate you on how finance can help make or break the deal.

This next section will give you an overview of options that are available. Let your team know how important it is for you to find the financing that fits your needs instead of making you fit the financing!

TYPES OF MORTGAGE LOANS

Your team can give you details on loan programs that might meet your needs. Take the time to ask questions and share your desires and goals. Do not be afraid to let them know if you do not understand a program the first time it is explained to you. Chances are they asked the same questions when they first learned about the program.

There are three standard loan programs (with variations):

1. FHA

2. VA

3. Conventional

The Federal Housing Administration (FHA) insures the lender against loss in the event a borrower defaults (stops making payments) on an FHA loan. The lender receives a guarantee against a percentage of loss on a VA loan from the Department of Veterans Affairs. A conventional loan is neither insured nor guaranteed by the government, so the down payment and qualifying guidelines are tougher than for FHA or VA loans. Some of the variations of these loans include:

Fixed-Rate Mortgages	*Adjustable-Rate Mortgages (ARMs)*
30-year fixed	6-month ARMs
15-year fixed	1-year ARMs
Balloons	3-year ARMs
Buydowns	5-year ARMs (also 7-year and 10-year)

Fixed-Rate Mortgages

Fixed-rate mortgages have a fixed interest rate, a fixed monthly payment, and are completely paid off over the term of the loan (usually 15 or 30 years).

A portion of the monthly payment goes toward the interest due on the loan and the remaining portion goes toward reducing the principal balance.

During the first ten years on a 30-year fixed-rate loan, more than 84 percent of the monthly payment is applied to interest. The only good news is that interest is deductible from your income tax. It is not until the 22nd year that 50 percent of the principal balance is paid off.

On a 15-year fixed-rate loan, the payments are higher than 30-year fixed-rate loans but the principal is paid off much faster. Approximately 50 percent of the principal balance is paid off in the first nine years.

For those who want the lower monthly payment of a 30-year fixed-rate loan but who would still like to reduce the term on the loan, there is another option. Lenders allow additional payments to be made directly to the principal. Those checks should be written separately from your monthly payment and clearly marked "apply to principal."

If you were to make one extra payment each year, applied directly to the principal, a 30-year loan could be paid off in 19 to 22 years, depending on when the payment is applied. Payments can be made in one lump sum or can be spread out with small additional payments made with each monthly payment.

This is a good option for some people because if a financial emergency does come up the buyer is not locked into the higher payment of the 15-year loan.

Balloon Mortgages

Balloon mortgages allow buyers to obtain slightly lower interest rates than fixed-rate mortgages but they are not fully amortized (paid off over the life of the loan).

Instead of a 30-year term, the outstanding principal is called due at a specific time prior to the 30-year period. Typical terms are 5-, 7-, or 10-year terms.

Statistics show us that the average American moves every three to five years. If you know you will be transferred or simply will want to move in less than five to seven years you can save money on interest with a balloon loan instead of paying the higher interest on a fixed-rate loan.

❗BEWARE

● Any time you are considering anything other than a fixed-rate loan, you should request a copy of the program description or a disclosure on the loan. Always make sure the details on the loan are spelled out in detail and ask for explanations of anything not understood.

Federal law requires disclosures to be given within three days of loan application. But it makes more sense for you to make sure you fully understand your loan choices before you purchase a home.

A lot of time and money can be wasted if you shop for a home based on a loan program with a lower interest rate than fixed rates available and then decide you are not comfortable with the loan terms after you make your loan application.

Adjustable-Rate Mortgages (ARMs)

Adjustable-rate mortgages (ARMs) have interest rates and payments that change over the life of the loan. The interest rate is adjusted to match the rise or fall of a preselected interest rate index. The buyer's regular payments will increase or decrease accordingly.

Many buyers prefer an ARM because the initial rate of the ARM is usually 2 percent or more lower than a fixed-rate mortgage. Another advantage is that, if rates go down, you do not have to refinance but will have your payment adjusted according to current rates on your adjustment date.

The adjustment date varies according to the type of loan you originated. Typical adjustment dates include six month, one year, three year, and five year. Some ARMs combine two adjustment periods. For example, a 5/1 ARM has a fixed rate for the first five years and then adjusts annually for the remaining life of the loan.

Make sure you read the program description and/or the disclosure carefully. Other key elements of an ARM to consider are:

- *Note rate.* The first year's interest rate (unless a teaser rate is offered) on which first year and life caps are calculated.

- *Teaser rate.* An initial rate offered for the first 6 to 12 months, which is sometimes substantially lower than the fully indexed rate on the loan.

- *Caps.* Limits placed on payments, interest rates, and/or the balance of the loan. Caps can limit increases by either a dollar amount or a percentage. Typical caps include an annual cap of 1 percent to 2 percent and a lifetime cap of 4 percent to 6 percent. An annual cap limits the amount of the increase each year. The life time cap limits the amount of the increase over the life of the loan.

- *Index.* A measurement used by lenders to determine changes to the interest rate charged on ARMs. The index reflects the current cost of money. If the index goes up or down, the interest rate increases or decreases according to the caps in place.

A fully indexed rate is the real interest rate. As the interest rate adjusts, it always adjusts to the fully indexed rate as long as that rate is under the designated caps on the loan.

Let us take an example of an ARM rate with the first year or teaser rate of 6 percent. The loan is convertible at the Fannie Mae published rate of 7.71 plus .625 percent. The caps are 2 percent and 6 percent and the margin is 3 percent. The index is the One Year Treasury Security (margin + index = fully indexed rate).

Let us say rates are stable and you get this loan because all the lender tells you is that you can get this great ARM rate at 6 percent. Everything is great and the first change comes up. The servicing lender takes the one-year Treasury Security index of 4.63 percent and adds the margin of 3 percent and low and behold you have a second year rate of 7.63 percent, which is the fully indexed rate. This is not such a great deal when you could have secured a 30-year fixed rate of 6.625 percent.

ARMs are only a good option when you can get the fully indexed rate well below what a fixed rate would be at the time you get the loan. Most of the time there are better options than ARMs.

The index can be set by the government or by private lending institutions and is based on published, independent financial data.

Common indexes are:

- Treasury Bill (T-Bill) Index. This is calculated weekly by the Federal Reserve using the sales price of Treasury bills and Treasury securities.

- 11th District Cost of Funds Index (COFI). This is based on a group of thrifts in California, Arizona, and Nevada. To calculate their index, they add their monthly interest expenses and divide that number by their average monthly balance of certain liabilities.

- London Interbank Offer Rates Index (LIBOR). This is calculated using the interest rates offered by six major European banks to their largest customers (similar to the prime rate in the United States).

- *Margin.* This represents the lenders' cost of doing business, plus profit. The margin is added to the index on the adjustment date to calculate the new payment for the coming period. The margin is identified when the loan is originated and will remain the same for the life of the loan.

- *Convertibility.* This is the ability to convert to a fixed rate during a specified time period. The disclosure will tell you if the ARM is convertible, the time period it is allowed, and how much it might cost.

- *Assumability.* Some ARMs allow the loan to be assumed by a qualified buyer. This can be an advantage if rates have gone up and also can allow buyers to assume the loan with little to no equity, depending on the situation of the seller and the property.

❗ BEWARE

Negative amortization can occur when the combination of interest rate adjustments and payment caps results in monthly payments that do not cover the monthly interest due. This means your payment may have a cap that prevents the payment from increasing but the unpaid interest is added to the loan amount. When an ARM has a payment cap, that should be a red flag to you that negative amortization can occur.

Some buyers may feel that the risk of negative amortization is acceptable if it will get them into a home they could not otherwise qualify for. Just make sure you read your disclosure carefully and consider reviewing it with an attorney and/or financial consultant.

Buydowns

Fixed-rate loans can be combined with buydowns to reduce the interest rate and the monthly payments. Permanent buydowns reduce the buydown for the life of the loan. Here's an example:

Rebekah and Ron Petrucci found their dream home. They wanted a loan of $125,000 but did not want their principal and interest (P&I) payment to be more than $835. Current interest rates were at 8 percent. By paying discount points (one point equals 1 percent of the loan amount) they could buy the interest rate down to 7 percent for a P&I payment of $831.

The cost for a permanent buydown varies according to daily interest rates and can be expensive. For instance, if it cost four points to buydown the Petrucci's loan, that would cost $5,000.

Another option is for a temporary buydown. A temporary buydown buys the interest rate down temporarily for a set number of years. For example:

If the Petrucci's only needed their payments to be below $835 per month for the first year, they could obtain a 2-1 buydown. With a fixed note rate of 8 percent, a 2-1 buydown would allow them to make P&I payments at 6 percent the first year (2 percent below the note rate), 7 percent the second year (1 percent below the note rate), and then years 3 to 30 they would pay the note rate of 8 percent.

The temporary 2-1 buydown would cost the Petrucci's approximately 2.5 percent of their loan amount. That means instead of paying $5,000 for a permanent buydown they would pay $3,125.

With a loan amount of $125,000 and a note rate of 8 percent, the monthly payments would look like this:

Year 1	@ 6%	P&I	$749.43
Year 2	@ 7%	P&I	$831.62
Years 3–30	@ 8%	P&I	$917.20

Temporary buydowns can be for different time frames, such as a 3-2-1 buydown. The 2-1 buydown, the most common, is the most cost effective for two reasons:

1. The cost for the 3-2-1 is a lot higher than a 2-1 buydown because you are buying it down for three years instead of two and by 3 percent for the first year instead of 2 percent.

2. Most lenders allow buyers to qualify at no more than 2 percent below the note rate on FHA, VA, and conventional loans. (In some states VA buyers still qualify at the note rate. Always check with your local lender.)

Anyone can pay for the temporary 2-1 buydown. The seller, the buyer, a builder, a gift from a family member, or even the lender if the buyer is willing to take an interest rate above par pricing. (This is premium pricing and will be explained later in this chapter.)

Many sellers and builders would rather pay for the buydown than accept less for the home than the listing price. When sellers contribute for the buydown, they can help buyers qualify to purchase their home when the buyer may not have been able to without a buydown.

A 2-1 temporary buydown can make as much as a $15,000 to $50,000 difference in the loan amount a buyer can qualify for depending on the interest rate and the loan amount. These fees also can be tax deductible. (Sellers, builders, and buyers should consult with their accountants to determine the tax benefits.)

Stop! Don't Reduce That Sales Price!

Reducing your sales price should be a last resort. Consider the leverage you can gain through financing options. If you can lower the interest rate for the buyer, you effectively lower the amount the buyer pays for the home by reducing the amount of interest that will be paid. A lower interest rate also makes it easier for buyers to qualify and opens up the market to more buyers.

What is the first thing most people do when their house does not sell right away? Reduce the sales price, right? How much does reducing the payment of a $100,000 house by $2,500 change the monthly payments? Less than $20 per month. The question then becomes, will that amount make a difference in the number of buyers who can buy your home? *NO!*

What if you could take that same $2,500 and change the payments by $140 to $150 a month, depending on the note rate? Now you are opening up the market to many of the buyers who are "ready and willing" but may not have been "able" to buy your

HOW TO CALCULATE A TEMPORARY 2-1 BUYDOWN

Loan Amount:	$100,000	
Note Rate:	9%	Note Rate P&I: $805
Interest Rate 1st Year:	7%	1st Year P&I: $665
Interest Rate 2nd Year:	8%	2nd Year P&I: $733
Interest Rate Years 3–30:	9%	3–30 Year P&I: $805

$805	–	$665	=	$140	× 12 =	$1,680
Note Rate P&I		1st Year P&I		Monthly Difference		1st Year Buydown Cost

$805	–	$734	=	$71	× 12 =	$852
Note Rate P&I		2nd Year P&I		Monthly Difference		2nd Year Buydown Cost

$1,680	+	$852	=	$2,532
Cost 1st Year		Cost 2nd Year		Total Cost of Buydown

* Some lenders may charge a fee of .75 percent for buydowns on FHA or VA loans house. Your team can do this as long as your house will appraise at the price you have it listed at.

When you look at the buydown example on the previous page, you will see that the monthly difference in the first year P&I payment and the note rate P&I payment is $140 per month. The lender will qualify the buyer at the first year note rate plus taxes and insurance (except VA loans in some states).

The total cost of the buydown was $2,532. Spending the $2,500 this way instead of reducing the price may help the seller reach buyers who may not have been able to purchase the house otherwise.

Not every buyer is a candidate for a buydown. Lenders look for upward mobility in income such as future raises, promotions, completing education, children graduating from college, etc. A buydown also may work for a buyer who has a large monthly payment on a debt that will be paid off in a year or two.

SELLER CONTRIBUTIONS

As long as a house will appraise at the price it is listed at, a seller may want to help pay some of the buyers closing costs instead of reducing the price. Seller contributions are allowed on FHA, VA, and conventional loans.

Do you remember the two most common barriers to homeownership?

1. Down payment

2. Closing costs

Compare the following with an 8 percent interest rate and closing costs estimated at 3.5 percent of the loan amount:

Option 1. Seller reduces price by $3,000 so that the buyer will have a loan amount of $97,000 instead of $100,000.

Loan Amount	Closing Costs	P&I Payment
$100,000	$3,500	$733.76
− 97,000	− 3,395	− 711.75
$ 3,000	$ 105	$ 22.01

The buyer now pays $3,395 in closing costs, a savings of $105. The monthly P&I payment is now $711.75, a savings of $22 a month. This option does not do a lot for helping more buyers qualify for a loan, does it?

Option 2. Seller contributes $3,000 toward the buyers' closing costs on a loan amount of $100,000.

Loan Amount	Closing Costs		P&I Payment
$100,000	Buyer	$ 500	$733.76
	Seller	3,000	
		$3,500	

In Option 1, the buyer paid $3,395 in closing costs. In Option 2, the buyer only pays $500 in closing costs, a savings of $2,895. The P&I payment in Option 2 will be $22 more but that is not enough to affect the buyer's qualifying ratios. If the buyer has less closing costs to pay, that will give her more money to pay toward her down payment.

Option 2 has just helped the buyer overcome the two most common barriers to home ownership and has helped a seller open up the market to more buyers who are now "able" to purchase their home.

Sellers who reduce the sales price simply lose the amount of money they reduced it by. If the sellers contribute to the buyers' closing costs, the amount gets lumped into the cost of selling the home and there may be tax advantages available to the seller (check with your accountant for details).

The key to using finance incentives over reducing the sales price is that the home must be able to appraise at the listed price. If the house is overpriced, it would be better to reduce the sales price and then consider finance incentives.

You also will need to check the loan guidelines to see how much the seller is allowed to contribute. The contributions the seller is allowed to pay for the buyer depend on the following:

- Type of loan

- Loan-to-value ratio (LTV is loan amount ÷ sales price)

- Owner occupied or investor

Standard Allowable Contributions

Type of Loan   Contribution Allowed

FHA   6% of the sales price

VA   Up to 4% above normal costs paid by seller. Normal costs include flood determination, document preparation fees, underwriting fees, all of escrow fee, and final inspections, if any.

Conventional   95% LTV: 3%
               90% LTV and below: 6%
               Investor: 2%

If sellers do not want to contribute to the buyers' closing costs, they can use premium pricing and allow the lender to pay part of the buyers' closing costs, which will free up more money for the down payment.

Premium Pricing/Above Par Pricing

Are you short on cash for closing? Will you be moving in a few years? What would it mean to you if you could come up with a few thousand more dollars without having to give it away as a seller, or asking the buyer to borrow it, sell off possessions, or ask family members to give it to you? Or, if you know you will be moving again in a few years, what if you could pay less closing costs and keep more money in the bank? The answers to the questions above should tell you that finance really is the key to buying and selling real estate!

One way to cut down on out-of-pocket expenses and keep more money in your pocket is to consider the advantages of premium pricing. With premium pricing, the lender can pay part of the buyers' closing costs. To compensate the lender, the buyer pays a slightly higher interest rate. Some lenders refer to this as above par pricing (above 0 discount points).

If par pricing were at 8 percent, the quote would look like this: 8% 0 + 1. Zero discount points plus one origination fee (1 percent of the loan amount). Above par pricing would be any interest rate above 8 percent and would look something like this: 8.5% (2) + 1. This example shows a *credit* of 2 percent of the loan amount plus one origination fee.

On a $50,000 loan, a credit of 2 percent would equal $1,000; on a $100,000 loan, a credit of 2 percent would equal $2,000. As you can see, the higher your loan amount the more premium pricing is available. That can be a lot of money left over to pay closing costs or to keep in the bank in case of an emergency.

Ask your real estate team how much money is available for premium pricing? Premium pricing varies on a daily basis, according to current interest rates.

Not all lenders understand how important premium pricing can be to increasing home ownership. If you can help buyers reduce the closing costs, that leaves them more money left over for a down payment.

The following buyers are good candidates for premium pricing:

- Buyers who are short on cash

- Buyers who know they will move in a few years

- Buyers with 401K plans

Consider the following example:

Should the Savages take an interest rate at par pricing or should they consider premium pricing?

Valery and Gary Savage purchased a home for $283,750 with a loan amount of $227,000. Par pricing is at 8 percent. 8.5 percent has 2.5 percent premium available. Closing costs are approximately $11,350. The Savages will be transferred in three years and Valery had a 401K plan at work that her employer matches dollar for dollar. They have enough money for closing costs and the down payment, with money left over after closing.

P&I payment @ 8.5%	$1,745.43
P&I payment @ 8%	1,665.64
Difference in P&I	79.79

To answer the question, simply take the dollar amount of premium pricing that is available and divide it by the difference in P&I payments at 8 percent and 8.5 percent.

Loan Amount	$227,000
Premium Pricing	× 2.5%
	$ 5,675 ÷ 79.79 = 71

This tells us that if the Savages took the 8 percent rate and paid $5,675 in closing costs instead of using premium pricing to pay that amount of their closing cost, they would have to be in their home at least 71 months before they would break even.

In other words, the P&I payment at 8 percent would have saved them $2,872.44 over the 36 months they plan to be in the home. But they would have paid $5,675 up front in closing costs that could have been paid with premium pricing. That is a loss of $2,802.56. Do not forget that some of the higher payment due to the 8.5 percent interest rate also would have had tax deductions on the interest because interest is tax deductible.

Also consider that Valery had a 401k plan at work that her employer matched dollar for dollar. What if she had been able to take the $5,675 she did not have to pay in closing costs and put it into her 401K plan? The money would have doubled.

The following questions should help narrow the choices for the type of loan that would best suit the buyer:

- How long does the buyer expect to live in the new home?

- Is there expectation of upward mobility or decrease of income?

- Is anyone else other than the borrower contributing toward closing costs?

- Is there expectation for increase or decrease in debt?

- What is the buyer's comfort zone for monthly payments and/or increase in payments?

Flexible Loan Programs

Keep in mind that there are loan programs for almost every credit situation. There are even conventional loans that allow $0 down payment (100% LTV). These loans usually require very good credit with high credit scores, but they even can allow some of the closing costs to be rolled into the loan. The rates are not as high as you would think either.

Self-employed? No problem! How about a no doc loan (no documentation)? These loans vary from no income verification needed to no employment verification needed, and usually do not use ratios to determine the maximum payment allowed. Stated income loans use the income stated on loan application. These loans are helpful to self-employed people who usually have to average their income for the past two years and who may be making a lot more money this year than they were last year. The point is that just about anyone who really wants to own a home has the opportunity to do so with all of the loan options available today. The key is to find an honest, ethical REALTOR® or lender that will take the time to educate you on your options.

Mortgage insurance protects the lender if the buyer fails to repay the loan. The government and private mortgage insurance companies have made it possible for buyers to purchase a home with a lower down payment than would be required by a conventional loan at conventional terms.

MORTGAGE INSURANCE

Private Mortgage Insurance (PMI)

If a buyer puts less than 20 percent down on a standard conventional loan, the lender will require PMI. With PMI, the buyer can put as little as 3 percent down.

- On a $230,000 home, instead of putting $46,000 down, a buyer could invest as little as $6,900.

- On a $75,000 home, instead of putting $15,000 down, a buyer could invest as little as $2,250 (100 percent LTVs have higher PMI requirements).

The cost of PMI varies according to the type of loan the buyer chooses and the geographic location of the property. The lender on your team can give you a chart of PMI rates in your area.

PMI charges will be added to your monthly mortgage payments and your closing costs or may be added to your loan amount. Your lender can review your options with you.

A common way to avoid PMI is with a second lien. Fannie Mae and Freddie Mac do not require mortgage insurance (MI) if your combined LTV (loan-to-value) is 75 percent and you put at least 10 percent down. For instance, on a $100,000 sales price, you put down 10 percent, the lender arranges for a second lien for $15,000 and the first lien is $75,000. You have put 10 percent down and avoided MI. The second rate is higher than the first and the term normally is only for 15 years. The benefit is that the interest is tax deductible, the second pays off sooner than the first, and if you want to prepay a portion of your loan you can pay the second off and you get the benefit of the decrease in payment sooner than with one loan. Most nonconforming investors will waive the MI with a combined LTV of 80 percent (i.e., a first for 80 percent, a second for 10 percent and 10 percent down).

Here are some frequently asked questions about PMI.

Q: What is private mortgage insurance?

A: PMI is a type of insurance that helps protect lenders against a homeowner defaulting on his or her mortgage. This insurance protection, provided by a private mortgage insurance company, covers loans that tend to be associated with default risk, including low down payment loans and some of today's modern mortgage products. In effect, it supplements the borrower's reduced equity that would be available to cover a lender's loss if a borrower were to stop making payments.

Q: Do I have a choice in PMI companies?

A: While you will want to discuss the different payment plans with your lender, it is probably better to let your lender choose the PMI company. Most conventional loans with less than 20 percent down payment will need to meet the underwriting guidelines required by the lender and those required by the PMI company. Different PMI companies may have different guidelines. The lender will try to match your credit situation with the PMI company suited to your needs.

Q: What if I have a good credit rating and I can meet the monthly mortgage payments—am I obligated to have PMI?

A: Even when borrowers have an excellent credit record and the capability to meet mortgage payments, most lenders require PMI. PMI allows lenders to grant loans with lower down payments than they may have been willing to consider.

Q: Are PMI premiums paid over the life of the loan or can they be canceled at some point?

A: In most cases, the insurance is renewed annually at the option of the lender, usually until the loan is paid down to 80 percent of the original value of the property. At that point, the borrower may prove to the lender, usually by means of a current appraisal, that the loan balance is now 80 percent or less of the current value of the property and, therefore, request cancellation of the PMI. On July 29, 1998, a mortgage insurance cancellation law was signed into effect. It calls for automatic cancellation when home equity reaches 22 percent of the value of the property.

Q: Why would a lender be cautious about eliminating PMI?

A: In some areas of the country, depreciation (decrease in value) has caused serious problems with property valuation. For example, in Washington State in 1989 and 1990, homes were almost doubling in value due to the influx of California buyers. Once this slowed down, property values returned to normal and then started to decrease in value in some areas. If a lender drops the PMI on a property that decreases in value a few years later and then goes into foreclosure, the lender will take the complete loss.

Q: Can the lender cancel PMI and still collect the PMI insurance from the buyer?

A: No. That is called "loaded couponing" and is not allowed.

Q: What if I do not want to pay PMI?

A: If you do not want to pay PMI, you have several choices:

- You can put 20 percent or more down.

- You can put 10 percent down and obtain a 10 percent second lien from the seller or from a second lien mortgage company.

- You can try to find a "self-insuring" lender (a lender that insures its own loans or "portfolios" (does not sell loans off to the secondary market).

Q: What are the benefits of PMI?

A: Surveys have shown that the greatest barrier to home ownership is being able to come up with the down payment and the closing costs. PMI reduces the capital required to purchase a home. This allows millions of people to purchase homes much sooner than they would be able to if they had to wait until they could save 20 percent for a down payment.

Q: If you have the 20 percent down payment, is it always better to avoid PMI?

A: No. Sometimes it makes sense for a buyer to put less down with the help of PMI in order to have money left over for future expenses. According to MGIC, the nation's first long-term private mortgage guaranty insurer, PMI can give buyers financial flexibility.

Many buyers know they will have upcoming expenses, such as a wedding, college tuition, or a new car. They may plan to take out a home equity loan at a later date. However, home equity loans have higher interest rates than first liens and will have additional closing costs. It may be more economical to put less down with the help of PMI.

Mortgage Insurance Premium (MIP)

On FHA loans, the government insures the loan for the lender. The minimum down payment required is approximately 3 percent of the value of the house. (The value is the lower of sales price or the appraisal.)

In September 1983, FHA began collecting a Mortgage Insurance Premium (MIP) to offset defaulted loans. There is a one-time MIP (OTMIP) that can be added to the loan amount or paid in cash at closing. A seller also can pay the OTMIP for the buyer or it can be paid with a gift from a family member or a close family friend.

In July 1991, an additional premium was added. This is collected as a monthly premium (MMIP) and is added to the monthly payment on the house. Condominiums are exempt from the OTMIP, but owners do pay monthly premiums. The amount of the OTMIP and the amount and duration of the MMIP varies according to the down payment and the date the original loan was closed.

MIP is subject to change. The following chart has a blank for OTMIP you can fill in with current information from a local lender on your team or visit HUD's Web site at www. hud.gov.com.

FHA MORTGAGE INSURANCE PREMIUM CHART

Current OTMIP: _____ **Date:** _____

Loan Closing Date	Amount and Duration of Monthly MIP		
	LTV Less Than 90%	LTV 90% to 95%	LTV More Than 95%
Through 9/30/92	.50% for 5 years	.50% for 8 years	.50% for 10 years
10/1/92 to 9/30/94	.50% for 7 years	.50% for 12 years	.50% for 30 years
On or after 10/1/94	.50% for 11 years	.50% for 30 years	.55% for 30 years

MIP is subject to change. Verify current amounts with local lenders.

Notice that the higher the LTV, or lower the down payment, the longer the MMIP is required. The reason given for this is that loans with lower LTVs are more likely to go into default because the buyer has less invested, thus making it easier to walk away when times get rough.

If you are going to allow your buyer to assume your FHA loan, the chart above should be used to inform potential buyers of MMIP requirements. It also can be an advantage to a seller to have a home on the market that can be assumed with MMIP paid off or soon to be paid off, because this would reduce the monthly payment for potential buyers. Closing costs also usually are less on assumptions than on new loans.

Buyers that assume FHA loans obtain the loan at the interest rate currently on the loan. If this rate is below current interest rates, this also can give the seller a competitive edge over other homes in the area and allow the buyer a lower monthly payment.

Here are some frequently asked questions about MIP:

Q: If I put 20 percent down, do I have to pay MIP?

A: MIP is required regardless of the down payment.

Q: Can you exceed the maximum loan amount the lender will allow when you add the OTMIP to the loan amount?

A: Yes. Maximum loan amounts for conventional, FHA, and VA loans vary each year. Your local lender can give you the current maximum FHA loan amount. You then can add the OTMIP to that amount for your total loan amount. Your principal and interest (P&I) payment will be based off the total loan amount.

Q: If the OTMIP is for the life of the loan, do I get a refund if I pay the loan off early?

A: Yes. If the loan is not in default, the buyer may be entitled to a refund of the unused portion of the OTMIP. The lender who administers the loan payoff usually is the one who processes the refund paperwork. If you do not receive your OTMIP refund within 120 to 180 days, you may want to write the FHA at:

Mortgage Insurance Accounting
Insurance Operations Division, HUD
451 Seventh St., SW
Washington, DC 20410

Funding Fees

On VA loans, the government guarantees a portion of the loan for the lender. This can allow qualified veterans to purchase a home with no down payment requirement. The seller also can pay closing costs for the buyer.

Instead of mortgage insurance, there is a funding fee charged on all VA loans to help the government offset the cost of defaulted loans. The funding fee varies according to the down payment, first-time use of VA guarantee benefits, second or subsequent use, and to the type of duty of the veteran. The funding fee is waived for veterans with service-related disabilities.

Funding fees are subject to change, so the following chart has blanks for you to fill in with current information from a local lender on your team.

CURRENT VA FUNDING FEES			
Down Payment	Active Duty or Veterans	Guard or Reservists	Second or Subsequent
Less than 5%			
5% to less than 10%			
10% or more			

Consider these frequently asked questions about funding fees:

Q: Can someone pay the funding fee for the veteran?

A: Yes. Anyone can pay the funding fee. The buyer, the seller, a gift from a family member or close friend, or the fee can be financed into the loan.

Q: Can you exceed the maximum loan amount the lender will allow on a VA loan by adding the funding fee to the loan amount?

A: No. The funding fee can be added to the loan amount as long as it does not exceed the maximum loan amount the lender will allow. The lender on your team can give you current maximum loan amounts.

F.Y.I. Did you know:

- Ten percent of our population nationwide is now or has been at some time in the military? That is roughly 30 million people (according to estimates derived from data released in 1996 by the Department of Veterans Affairs).

- Two-thirds of them—approximately 21 million U.S. citizens—never have bothered to use their VA home loan entitlement?

Why? That is what John Ellis, a veteran and author of *Using Your VA Entitlement Home Buyer's Guide,* wanted to know. He found that it was because at least 8 million fellow veterans did not know how to apply for a VA home loan (about half of those are not even aware that they are eligible).

If you are a veteran and would like more information on VA entitlement, you can call the VA Home Hotline at 800-VA-HOMES. Or visit the VA Homes Internet Home Page at www.1800VAHomes. com. To contact a local VA regional office, call 800-827-1000.

ALTERNATIVES TO STANDARD LOANS AND PROGRAMS

The standard loans discussed in this book conform to secondary market guidelines. Keep in mind that some lenders have the ability to portfolio loans and may offer loans we have not discussed. Portfolio means to keep the loan in-house and not sell it off to the secondary market.

Lenders also have loans available for nonconforming and "jumbo" loans. A nonconforming loan simply means it has characteristics that do not conform to secondary market guidelines. A jumbo loan refers to a loan with a loan amount higher than the limit accepted by the secondary market.

Fannie Mae

Fannie Mae also has special loans available to help low-, moderate-, and middle-income borrowers purchase homes. Following is the company's mission statement:

Fannie Mae Mission Statement

Since its creation by Congress in 1938 and its evolution into a shareholder-owned company in 1968, Fannie Mae's mission has been to provide financial products and services that increase the availability and the affordability of housing for low-, moderate-, and middle-income Americans.

Fannie Mae believes that home ownership is the key to individual work and community values. With this in mind, it has launched the National Campaign for Consumer Education to Increase Home Ownership.

It developed a series of mortgage products, Community Lending Products, that are alternatives to standard loan programs. These mortgage products have been designed to help overcome the two common barriers to home ownership:

1. Down payment

2. Closing costs

Fannie Mae believes the key to increasing home ownership is to provide consumer education on the steps involved in buying a home and obtaining a mortgage, and responsibilities as a homeowner. Your real estate team can give you details on education programs available and on the following Fannie Mae community lending products:

- Community Home Buyer's Program

- 3/2 Option

- Fannie 97

- Community Home Buyer's Start-Up Mortgage

- Fannie Neighbors

- Community Seconds Mortgage Loans

- Lease-Purchase Mortgage Loans

- Community Land Trust Mortgage Loans

- Magnet 5 Employer-Assisted Housing Mortgage Loans

- Magnet 3/2 Employer-Assisted Housing Mortgage Loans

Habitat for Humanity

Habitat for Humanity is a great organization that works to put decent shelter on the hearts and minds of people everywhere. Habitat supporters believe that substandard housing and homelessness are politically, socially, and morally unacceptable. People, Christian and non-Christian alike, who are disturbed by this injustice and want to alleviate the housing crisis are invited to join in the work of Habitat.

Since its founding in 1976 by Millard and Linda Fuller, Habitat for Humanity International has built and rehabilitated some 80,000 houses with families in need. The Fullers developed the concept of partnership housing in the 1960s. The following letter will give you an idea of their vision:

> *What the poor need is not charity but capital, not caseworkers but coworkers. And what the rich need is a wise, honorable, and just way of divesting themselves of their overabundance. The Fund for Humanity will meet both of these needs. Money for the fund will come from shared gifts by those who feel they have more than they need and from non-interest bearing loans from those who cannot afford to make a gift but who do want to provide working capital for the disinherited. . . . The fund will give away no money. It is not a handout.*

Homes are built and sold to families in need with no profit and no interest. The families are required to invest a minimum amount of time and effort and have the opportunity to work side by side with volunteers to build their home. This concept is so successful because it allows families in difficult situations to contribute toward their dream of home ownership and take pride in the accomplishment. It also allows the volunteers an opportunity to help others and feel good about themselves.

Habitat has shown enormous growth and is now in all 50 states, the District of Columbia, and more than 60 countries. At least one house is built every hour of every day. You can get more information about applying for a Habitat home and about volunteering with Habitat through their Web site at www.habitat.org or by ordering books and other materials from Habitat headquarters in Americus, Georgia at 912-924-6935, ext. 2312 or 2140.

The Nehemiah Program®

Another program that more people need to be aware of that allows people to purchase a home with less money out of pocket is The Nehemiah Program. Nehemiah is a California 501 (3)(c) nonprofit housing corporation. Nehemiah is not a government subsided organization. If you can qualify for an FHA loan, but do not have the money for a down payment, Nehemiah can help. According to the organization:

> *Nehemiah was a biblical personality who led in the reconstruction of the wall surrounding Jerusalem. Like our namesake, we are engaged in rebuilding communities by providing affordable housing and home ownership. We believe that housing is a critical strand in the social fabric that holds our country together.*
>
> —Don Harris, President & Executive Director

The Nehemiah Program is a down payment assistance program in which participating Nehemiah lenders arrange for a 3 percent gift from Nehemiah for a qualified borrower in conjunction with an approved loan product to be used for down payment. These gift monies do not have to be repaid. The borrower will need to have 1 percent of the sales price either in reserves (money in a bank account) or paid into the transaction as closing costs or prepaids.

Buyers must qualify for an eligible loan program—any single-family mortgage loan product that allows charitable organizations to provide gift funds toward down payment and closing costs and has been approved by Nehemiah.

One approved loan product is an FHA loan. FHA guidelines allow charitable organizations to provide gift funds as "borrowers funds" toward down payment and closing costs. Nehemiah has obtained approval from HUD to gift these funds to qualified borrowers. Other loan programs may be approved, check with local lenders.

Buyers should follow these four steps to obtain a gift from Nehemiah:

1. Obtain preapproval from a participating Nehemiah lender.

2. Complete an approved home ownership education program.

3. Show 1 percent of the sales price in reserves or put into the transaction.

4. Purchase a Nehemiah participating property.

A participating property is a home owned by a seller who has entered into a Participating Home Agreement or a builder who has entered into an Affordable Housing Services Agreement with Nehemiah. Real estate agents interested in working with the Nehemiah program should obtain a Real Estate Professional Certification Form.

The seller must agree to provide the buyer with a home warranty with a two-year roof coverage (or a two-year roof certification) and "clear" pest report. The seller also agrees to pay a service fee to Nehemiah within three business days after closing.

Nehemiah is a minority-controlled faith-based charitable organization that has assisted more families to become homeowners than any other privately funded program, and has significantly increased the percentage of minorities that are able to purchase homes.

However, Nehemiah does face challenges with HUD that we all need to be aware of. In 1999, HUD proposed a rule that would eliminate the availability of gift funds provided by The Nehemiah Program. Don Harris, Nehemiah's president and executive director, needs our support in encouraging the government to continue to allow programs that encourage home ownership to all nationalities. The Nehemiah Web site has a section under "government affairs" that will show you easy steps to contact elected officials for those wishing to show their support for the program. You can locate The Nehemiah Program's Web site at www.nehemiahprogam.org.

SUMMARY

Taking the time to consider finance options available to you will not only save you time but also will show you how to put more money back into *your* pocket for a change! Options both buyers and sellers will want to consider include premium pricing, temporary buydowns, seller contributions, and the different types of loans that are available.

For more information on different types of loans, visit the following Web sites:

- www.fanniemae.com

- www.hud.gov.com

- www.habitat.org

- www.nehemiahprogram.org

The information in this chapter on Habitat for Humanity and The Nehemiah Program was obtained from their Web sites.

CHAPTER FIVE

Tips for Buying and Selling

This chapter will review tips for making educated decisions in the home buying and selling process. Marketing tips and checklists are provided to help you set goals and avoid costly mistakes you might make in the "heat of the moment." Many times buyers and sellers get ripped off because they allow emotion to rule their decisions on pricing their home or negotiating the price or the financing. After reading this chapter you will be able to

- use checklists to help you make educated decisions on buying and selling.

- understand "For Sale By Owner" options.

- apply Boyd's Fast Track Marketing System to help you reduce the time your home is on the market.

Buying and selling real estate can be a very emotional process for a lot of people. Sellers may have put a lot of "blood, sweat, and tears" into their home and feel that they should be compensated for all they have done to improve the property. Buyers may feel that the seller is making too much money on the home or may not like some of the improvements the seller has made to the home. The bottom line is that real estate is too important to let emotion get in the way of making educated decisions. Taking the time to consider exactly what your wants, needs, and desires are before you start the process can save you time and money in the long run.

Boyd's Fast Track Marketing System

Everyone who has sold a home knows that the longer a home is on the market, the less you are likely to get for it. One of the first questions a buyer asks is how long the house has been on the market. Most believe that if it did not sell in the first 60 days then the seller will be more likely to take a low offer, especially in a seller's market. After all, buyers have not been beating the door down with offers if it has not sold yet.

At the same time, the longer a buyer takes to find a home and obtain financing, the more it could cost. The price of homes and interest rates could go up. When interest rates increase, the loan amount the buyer qualifies for goes down and the more the house will cost over the life of the loan. Consult the seller's and/or buyer's checklists to make the process go smoother and take less time.

SELLER'S FAST TRACK CHECKLIST

❑ Put your reasons for selling in writing.

❑ Determine if you will sell by owner or list with an agent.

❑ Build your real estate service team by reviewing Chapter 1 and using the questions provided to interview your team.

❑ Determine how much money you need to move into your new home, including down payment, closing costs, and moving costs. Do not forget to include the cost of setting up new utilities. Your agent or lender can help you estimate these costs and even can start the loan preapproval process for you.

❏ Calculate your bottom line by deducting your mortgage plus approximate closing costs for your area. Closing costs may be up to 4 percent plus another 5–8 percent if you list with a real estate company. (Your local title company or real estate agent can provide estimates.)

❏ Determine when you need to close.

❏ Set a goal for receiving an acceptable offer based on how long it takes in your market to have a buyer make loan application and have papers prepared for closing. If the turn-around time is 30 days, then you know you need to have an acceptable offer a minimum of 30 days before you need to close. You may want to give yourself an extra 15 days in case the deal falls through and you need to look for another buyer.

❏ Determine a realistic price range that will help you meet your goals. A real estate agent can give you a market evaluation showing you homes currently on the market and those that have sold in the past six months. You should also take the time to look at other homes in your neighborhood that are similar to your home. It helps to know what the competition has to offer and then figure out a way to give your property an edge over the competition. Financing incentives are one way to do this.

❏ Offer buyer financing incentives by reviewing Chapter 3. Many buyers are "ready and willing," but the more you can do to help them become "able," the faster you will close. Consider pricing your home so that you can offer at least 2.5 percent of the sales price toward closing costs for the buyer.

(continued)

❑ Review Chapter 4 and have the lender on your team prepare a mortgage comparison sheet to show buyers financing options, including 100 percent LTVs, temporary 2-1 buydowns, premium pricing options to reduce closing costs, loans for those with credit problems, etc.

❑ Prepare the property for showing—clean, repair, replace as needed. Ask title companies for brochures such as "51 Home Tips from Chicago Title" or visit <u>owner.com</u> on the Internet for a four-page seller checklist.

❑ Make sure you are familiar with fair housing laws so that you do not discriminate against potential buyers. Contact HUD's housing discrimination hot line at 800-669-9777 or have your agent review the fair housing laws in your area.

❑ Prepare seller disclosures required in your state. Your real estate team can provide these for you.

❑ Review safety procedures you can take when your house is on the market. Local law enforcement organizations may be able to visit with you to review precautions you can take to protect yourself and your home.

❑ Consider "round robin bidding" or the auction approach. Round robin bidding allows for open bids to be made on the property and bidding continues among the bidders until no one wants to top the highest bidder. In other words it continues "around the circle of bidders" until one bidder out bids all others. This can be done live or on the telephone. The key to making this work is total honesty. Many like this approach over closed bids where you give your bid privately one time without knowing what the others are bidding. You may bid more than you have to with closed bidding because you are afraid someone will outbid you.

The concept of bidding or auctions is great. But it is not for everyone. Some people may not feel comfortable handling the showings and facilitating the round robin. Many do not have the time to invest in preparing all the details either. If you are like most sellers and you do not want to deal with having your home on the market any longer than you have to, consider having your real estate service team—discussed in Chapter 1—study this approach. They can work with you to create a unique marketing plan based on the round robin approach. (Your agent should check with her or his real estate commission on your state's guidelines regarding round robin bidding or auctions.)

The Internet is starting to make bidding and auctions more popular. One site you may want to check out is www.homebid.com.

Ideas for Sellers to Consider

- Use a 12-day plan. The ad goes in the paper on Wednesday, with an open house scheduled the second weekend. Many people do not look at the real estate ads until Friday and this gives them another week to see the ad and plan to attend your open house. It also would allow them time to view the home and arrange a proxy to bid for them if they were not available on the bidding date.

- Have the team take calls and offer free loan consulting and preapprovals so interested buyers know exactly how high they can bid.

- Have buyer financing incentives included to open up the market to more buyers.

- Put a notice on flyers handed out that buyer's agents (agents representing the buyer only) are welcome and that if an agent is used, the buyers are responsible for paying for their agent's commission or that it can be added to the final bid.

- Have the lender on your team present at the open house with a laptop so he or she can pull credit reports and check credit scores for buyers who have not been preapproved. They could even provide Desktop Underwriting and possibly have the buyer preapproved before the bidding starts. Let everyone know that preapproved buyers will be given priority.

> NOTE: Some proponents of round robin bidding feel prequalification is not important because you have backup bidders. But what happens if the top three all fall through? If you have to go through the process a second time, you are likely to get offered a lot less because people will be suspicious of why it did not work the first time. Just make sure your lender provides several mortgage comparison sheets showing financing to fit every credit situation. With technology these days, it is fast and easy to check credit. Why not eliminate the problem before it exists?

- Decide if you will accept bids from a buyer who has a house to sell. If you decide you will, make sure you have the real estate agent on your team meet with the buyer to determine the marketability of the buyer's home. Some may decide this is too much of a risk and the whole point of this approach is for a quick sale. That is entirely up to the individual. Others may decide they could get a higher price and feel that if they let the bidders in second place know about the contingency and set a time limit on it, it could lessen the risk.

For Sale By Owners

For sale by owners are known to real estate professionals as FSBOs, and are often misunderstood. A lot of buyers think the reason the sellers are trying to sell their own home is because they had it on the market with a real estate professional and could not sell it. Bargain hunters often think they are desperate to sell and will take any offer. Many real estate agents think a FSBO's only goal is to save paying a commission.

The truth is that many FSBOs feel that they know their own home better than anyone else. And they want to at least have the opportunity to try to sell it themselves before they commit to listing it with just one company.

If you think about it, isn't that fair? If sellers want to try to sell their own home, they should have the right to do so without a lot of people trying to tell them all the reasons why they cannot do it.

Unfortunately, a lot of real estate agents and loan officers have been trained that the way to do business with a FSBO is to tell them why it is not a good idea for them to try to sell their own home. They come armed with all the reasons why the seller should list it with a real estate company.

It is true that being a FSBO is not a good idea for every seller. But at the same time it may be a good idea for some. This does not mean that real estate agents and FSBOs cannot work together if the FSBO does not list their home.

Friendly, productive relationships can exist between real estate agents and FSBOs without the agent taking the listing. Experience has shown that there is a lot a real estate agent can do for a FSBO without taking the listing. In return, the FSBO can do some things for the real estate agent that will make it worth the time and effort.

The first two steps in building productive relationships between FSBOs and real estate agents are to recognize the following:

1. Sellers have the right to sell their own home if that is what they want to do.

2. Real estate agents are in the business to list and sell real estate, but they also want to build long-term relationships that result in referrals and future business.

Services that a real estate agent can provide without taking a listing include:

- Help FSBO purchase a new home.

- Refer FSBO to an agent out of town.

- Prepare mortgage comparison sheets.

- Prepare a market evaluation and seller's net sheet to help the FSBO select the best price for their home.

- Prequalify potential buyers.

- Help FSBO and potential buyers obtain financing.

- Provide a "FSBO kit" (folder with helpful information for selling a home in the local market, which includes disclosures, brochures from title companies & lenders, tips on selling a home, etc.).

- Work out a one-time listing agreement. (This is usually a 24- to 48-hour agreement that allows the agent to show the house to a specific buyer and to receive a commission if the FSBO accepts the offer. The commission can be paid for by the FSBO or by the buyer. Most agents have special listing agreements for one-time showings, or you can have your attorney draw one up for you.)

- Help potential buyers sell their own homes so that they can purchase the FSBOs house faster.

In return for these services, FSBOs can

- purchase their new home from the agent.

- refer buyers not qualified or not interested to the agent for other properties and loan options.

- refer neighbors, coworkers, or family members who are thinking about selling or buying.

- recommend that buyers interested in their house who have their own home to sell before they can close work with the agent for a faster sale.

- allow the agent to bring interested buyers on a one-time listing basis.

As you can see, there are benefits for both the FSBO and the agent in this type of relationship. An added bonus is that if the FSBO does not sell their home and decides to list it with a real estate company, you both will know if you make a good team.

You may be bombarded by calls from brokers or agents telling you all the reasons you should list your home with them. Be prepared to talk with them and let them know the parameters you are willing to work under. For instance, you might start out by simply saying, *"I am not interested in listing my house right now but I would be willing to talk to you about a one-time, open listing agreement for a specific buyer."*

Or tell them you are not interested in listing your home but you do need counseling and help with financing for your new home as well as counseling for potential buyers. You quickly will weed out the agents who are only interested in taking your listing and will have the opportunity to meet honest, hard working, real estate professionals who respect your right to sell your home yourself.

It is to your advantage to have agents give you a full presentation when they do meet with you. Agents should present the services they can provide if you decide you want to sell your own home, then present the services they can provide should you decide to list your home with them.

After the full presentation, you will have valuable information on what you need to do to obtain the best price for your home. Then you can make an educated decision about putting your home on the market as a FSBO without feeling pressured to list with the agent. You also will know what additional services you will receive if you do decide to list with a particular agent.

Many FSBOs have a set time limit for how long they are willing to try selling their house by themselves. If the property does not sell in the time they desire, this approach is a great way to determine which agent would make a good addition to their team.

Buying a For Sale By Owner Property

Purchasing a home directly from the seller may save you money. You do need to make sure that if you purchase a home directly from a FSBO without counseling from a real estate professional that you consult an attorney, a title company, and/or a closing agent about legal issues regarding the proper transfer of property in your area.

Some buyers feel that they can get a better buy through dealing direct with the FSBO, but that is not always the case. Your real estate agent may be able to save you time and money through contacts with lenders, appraisers, title companies and closing agents. The agent also can make sure you get the proper disclosures about the condition of the home and that all of the legal paperwork is handled correctly.

Buyers should feel comfortable talking to their real estate agents about FSBO properties. The agent can show comparable properties in the neighborhood to help get a feel for the price range available. The agent also can meet with the FSBO (if no working relationship currently exists) and possibly arrange to show the property.

If you have a written agreement with the agent to represent you as the buyer, the agent also can be helpful in negotiating the best price for the property for you. Many agents are willing to enter into *buyer representative* contracts, which allow them to look out for the best interest of the buyer instead of representing the seller.

Either the seller or the buyer can pay the commission for these services. Laws regarding representation vary by state and are one of the first issues that should be addressed when buyers and sellers build their real estate teams.

❗ BEWARE

⬤ As we said at the beginning of the chapter, buying and selling real estate can be a very emotional experience. As a seller you also may have a lot of happy memories raising your family there.

On the other hand, you may need to sell because you have lost your job, gotten a divorce, or have health problems that prevent you from maintaining your home. If you are selling due to financial reasons, you may be feeling desperate to find a buyer.

As a buyer you may be looking for the home of your dreams to raise your family or the perfect home for retirement. Or you may be transferred and feel pressured to find a home and get settled so you can focus on your new position.

Buyers need to make sure they do not cut corners or take short cuts to try to save money. It is easy to make friends with the FSBO and be tempted to simply take their word for things instead of having everything thoroughly checked out. It also may make it harder to negotiate the price if you have "bonded" with the sellers. Take Shirley Wright for example:

> Shirley and her mother were out driving around in the country one afternoon and found a FSBO Shirley could not resist. It was a 4,800 square foot log home on five acres. She was paying cash for the home but was also on a limited budget as she was retired and on a fixed income.
>
> The sellers were the nicest people you could ever want to meet. Mr. Brown showed her how he scheduled maintenance seasonally so that it made it easy to keep the property in good condition. He also carefully explained how the home was custom built and would last much longer than standard homes.
>
> When asked how they determined the price, they showed her all the money they had invested in making sure it was built with top-of-the-line materials. The house was absolutely beautiful. It was also $50,000 more than Shirley had planned to spend. It also was big enough that her mother could live with her and share expenses.

The sellers invited Shirley and her mother to stay for dinner. They put steaks on the grill and had dinner on the deck that overlooked a 68-acre lake that adjoined the property. By the end of the meal they felt like they had all been friends for years.

When Shirley mentioned it was a bit more than she had planned to spend, Mr. Brown told her how she could save money on some of the closing costs. She really did not need an inspection or an appraisal because she was paying cash. He also volunteered to pay for the title policy and to have his attorney draw up all of the necessary paperwork.

They closed two weeks later. All went well for the first couple of months except for a moldy smell they could not seem to get rid of in the mother's bedroom closet. The major problems did not start until winter set in. The fireplace had a major leak, water poured in the windows in the breakfast room, the moldy smell grew worse, and the mother's clothes started to mildew.

The final straw was when the floor in the mother's bedroom fell two inches and separated from the house. When Shirley had someone out to inspect the foundation, they told her that when the pier and beam foundation was built, the concrete pads were not connected to the beams that supported the floor. They also informed her that the previous sellers had shored it up before so they had to have known about it. When the problems with the breakfast room were looked into, they pulled the ivy away from the windows outside and found extensive dry rot. They were told that a home made of logs or wood should never have plants against the house.

The bid for making all of the repairs to the house was more than $75,000. Shirley could not afford that and had to sell the home. She made sure that all potential buyers were aware of the problems and had copies of the estimates for repair. She ended up selling the house for $60,000 less than she had paid for it. She also had spent more than $10,000 trying to make repairs before it got totally out of control.

This case was extreme, but even minor repairs really can cause problems for a homeowner. The point is to always make sure you have the house professionally inspected and have an appraisal on the home, even if it is not required. There also are home warranties that are available that will cover the cost of appliances, air conditioners, and heaters. These are usually one-year policies but some can be extended after the first year. The policies can be paid for by the buyer or by the seller.

NARROW YOUR CHOICES

As a buyer, you need to remember that time is of the essence. You do not want to look at every home that is on the market or take forever making up your mind about which house you see that you want to make an offer on. As mentioned earlier, the longer it takes you to find a home and make an offer, the more it could end up costing you in terms of price or interest you have to pay.

Make sure you understand what kind of market you are in. Ask your real estate agent if it is a seller's market or a buyer's market. A seller's market means there are more buyers available than homes available. A buyer's market means that there are more homes available than buyers. The old law of supply and demand will make a difference in what you end up offering on your home.

If you are in a seller's market, be prepared to know what you want, how much you can afford, get loan preapproval as soon as possible, and be ready to act fast. If the seller knows you have an approved loan, your offer may be accepted over another offer that has not made loan application yet. In some seller's markets there are "bidding wars" where several offers come in at the same time and the home often sells for more than its listed price.

Your goal is to always sell in a seller's market and buy in a buyer's market. Few will make this goal.

Anyway, in both types of markets you have the potential of interest rates going up and if rates go up, the loan amount the lender will allow you (or that you will be comfortable with) goes down. The sooner you find a property and lock in an interest rate, the better.

You can do a lot to reduce the time it takes to find just the right home by taking time up front to determine what features are most important to you, which ones you would like to have but could live without, and just as important, which features or characteristics you absolutely do not want.

Many agents will tell you that they have sold a good many homes to people with features they were told up front the buyer did not want. But many of those buyers have suffered buyer's remorse not long after moving in. The goal is not simply to find a home, but to find one you will be happy in for as long as possible. So take time to really consider your wants, needs, and desires before jumping in the car with a real estate agent to look at houses. Then be ready to make a decision as soon as you see the right house. The following worksheets can help you make educated decisions.

Using the Features List

For those of you used to planning your day, the Features List will seem familiar. When you plan your activities you typically have more tasks you need to do than you have time to accomplish them. The only way to get a handle on your day is to prioritize your tasks so that you can work on the most important ones first. Use the same concept with the following list by giving high, medium, and low priority to the features you want in your new home. Give a copy of this list to the agent you work with to narrow the search. Keep in mind that it is rare to find a home that has all of the features you would like to have. Taking the time to prioritize the features you want and don't want will help you focus on the features that are really most important to you instead of getting caught up in the emotion of the moment.

FEATURES LIST

Features List

Use this list to help you decide which features you want most in a home. Your agent will use this information to find homes you really want to see!

Name: _____

(check priority level)	High	Medium	Low	(check priority level)	High	Medium	Low
Style:				Heating/Air condition	☐	☐	☐
Age of home	☐	☐	☐				
SFR/Duplex/Triplex/Fourplex	☐	☐	☐	Pool	☐	☐	☐
Condo/Town home	☐	☐	☐	View	☐	☐	☐
				Gated Community	☐	☐	☐

Features:				**Location:**			
Architecture	☐	☐	☐	Distance to work	☐	☐	☐
1-story	☐	☐	☐	Near family/friends	☐	☐	☐
2-story	☐	☐	☐	Parks	☐	☐	☐
Split	☐	☐	☐	Bike/jogging trails	☐	☐	☐
Tri-level	☐	☐	☐	Country club/Assoc.	☐	☐	☐
Number of bedrooms	☐	☐	☐	Shopping	☐	☐	☐
Size of master bath	☐	☐	☐	Health clubs	☐	☐	☐
Formal dining/living	☐	☐	☐	Schools	☐	☐	☐
Fireplace	☐	☐	☐	Hospitals	☐	☐	☐
Family room	☐	☐	☐	Military base	☐	☐	☐
Eat-in kitchen	☐	☐	☐	Police	☐	☐	☐
Yard	☐	☐	☐	Fire Department	☐	☐	☐
Fence	☐	☐	☐				
Basement/Workshop	☐	☐	☐	**Other:**			
Garage	☐	☐	☐		☐	☐	☐

Score Cards

You also may want to use a score card to help you make decisions and narrow your choices. A score card is simply a page you carry on a clipboard with the information and possibly a picture of each home you will look at. Using the Ben Franklin method of "pros" on one side and "cons" on the other, you can keep track of what you like and do not like about each property.

Before you leave a property, try to take time to sit down in the living room or in the kitchen. Look around and imagine how your furniture would fit and how you would decorate. List on your score card what you like and do not like. Also make notes of any remodeling or repairs you would need to make before you would be comfortable in the home.

Now here is the key, before you leave the second property, sit down and again make notes. Before leaving the second property, ask yourselves, "If I had to purchase one of these two homes, which one would I chose?" After giving it some thought mark an x over the one you did not choose.

Are you getting the picture? Now you go on to the third house and follow the same procedure. Before you leave the third house, again ask, "If I had to purchase one of these two homes which one would I choose?" Do you see what will happen? You will always have your choice narrowed down to one home. At the end of the tour you only will have one home left to choose from. You may want to go back to that home for another look or you may be ready to make an offer!

Remember, once you have decided you want to buy a home "time is of the essence." That does not mean you should rush your search. Just that you should take steps that will save you time and money. If you have a good real estate agent and you communicate your needs, wants, and desires up front, you should not have to waste your time looking at homes that will not work for you. Focus your search only on those homes that have most of the features you marked as high and medium priority.

SCORE CARD

Listing Price: _____ Days on Market: _____

Address: _____

Age: _____ Sq. Ft: _____ Price/Sq. Ft. _____

Bedrooms: _____ Living Areas: _____ Baths: _____

Garage: _____ Workshop: _____

Finance Incentives: _____ Other: _____

Pros	Cons

Comments: _____

_____

_____

_____

_____

Preoffer Checklist

Before making an offer, consider some of the following:

❑ Are you in a buyer's market or seller's market?

❑ Prices of comparable homes in the neighborhood?

❑ Price per square foot?

❑ Time home has been on market?

❑ Taxes on property?

❑ Insurance?

❑ Utilities?

❑ Homeowners association dues?

❑ Restrictions? (Any improvements you want to make may need approval from a homeowners association. Make sure you ask before making an offer and get approval in writing from the homeowners association to avoid problems later.)

❑ Cost of maintenance needed (pool, yard, house, etc.)?

❑ Cost of repairs needed?

❑ Home warranty provided by seller?

❑ Future growth and plans for traffic flow? (Traffic to and from work.)

❑ Schools? (Keep in mind districts can change, especially if new schools built.)

❑ Crime, shopping, entertainment, etc.?

❑ Talk to neighbors and ask strengths/weaknesses of area?

❑ Seller financing provided?

GAIN LEVERAGE USING FINANCE TO NEGOTIATE PURCHASE AND SALES AGREEMENTS

Both buyers and sellers should consider negotiating with finance instead of holding out for the highest price or making low offers. Review loan options in Chapter 4 before negotiating an offer. Many times sellers and buyers just want to bargain over the price. You sometimes can have more leverage if you consider having the seller pay financing incentives instead of lowering the price. This is usually a better deal for the seller and the buyer. Remember seller financing incentives vary based on the type of loan and are as follows:

- VA Loans   4% of Sales Price

- FHA Loans   6% of Sales Price

- Conventional Loans 95% LTV   3% of Sales Price
                       90% LTV   6% of Sales Price
                       Investor   3% of Sales Price

A temporary 2-1 buydown costs approximately 2.5 percent of the loan amount when interest rates are 9 percent and below. That changes the monthly payment by approximately $140 a month on a $100,000 loan, or more than $260 a month on a $200,000 loan. Remembering that the buyer qualifies at the first-year rate, you can see that a seller can open up the market to more buyers by paying for the buydown instead of reducing the sales price. It also helps to apply the money to closing costs so buyers do not have to come up with as much money out of pocket.

So, next time you negotiate the price of a home, consider all of your options before you simply reduce the price or offer less for the home.

HELPFUL WEB SITES

These are just a few helpful Web sites on buying and selling a home.

buyowner.com   MicrosoftAdvisor.com
forsalebyowner.com   RealSelect.com
Realtor.com   HomeGain.com

FAST TRACK PLAN TO PAY OFF YOUR MORTGAGE EARLY

Many people would like to be able to save thousands in interest payments by obtaining a 15-year loan instead of a 30-year loan. Unfortunately, reducing the term for the loan also reduces the loan amount the lender may allow and also raises the monthly payment. There are some other options you may want to consider. Instead of a 15-year loan go ahead and obtain a 30-year loan.

Then you can either (1) make additional payments directly to the principal or (2) choose a biweekly payment plan.

Additional Payments Applied to the Principal

Most lenders allow you to make additional payments to your principal at any time. Your payment coupon even may have a blank to specify how much extra you are paying with each monthly payment that you want applied to the principal balance. Or you can opt to pay a lump sum directed to the principal at any time you choose. It is estimated that if you pay one extra payment equal to your total house payment at the beginning of each year you will pay a 30-year loan off in 19 years. If you make the same payment at the end of each year, you pay the loan off in about 21 years.

Consider writing two checks with one check clearly stating that it applies to the principal. There have been some instances when borrowers made extra payments and when the lender received them they put the extra money in the escrow account and did not apply it to the principal. By the time you find this out a lot of interest can accumulate!

You may want to look on the Internet for sites that allow you to look at amortization schedules. For instance, Home Loan Corporation's Web site has an amortization calculator that will let you specify how much you are thinking about paying toward principal. You can then calculate how much it will save you and when your loan will be paid off. You can visit their site at www.homeloancorp.com.

Biweekly Mortgages

Another option is biweekly mortgages. Some lenders allow you to make your payments every other week instead of just once a month. Because there are five weeks in two months out of the year, this results in one extra total house payment each year that is applied directly to the principal. This plan works well for those that feel they may not be disciplined enough to make that extra payment each year on their own.

SUMMARY

Following the seller and buyer checklists for fast track marketing and preoffer checklist can help buyers and sellers make educated decisions instead of decisions based on emotion. Emotional decisions often lead to costly mistakes.

When sellers and buyers use techniques to shorten the time it takes to sell or buy a home, they can save both time and money. Sellers can offer finance incentives and work with their team on creative marketing techniques such as round robin bidding. Buyers can use forms such as the features list and score card to help them focus on important details and not get sidetracked by minor issues.

Whether you will work with an agent is a personal choice based on your needs, wants, and desires. The bottom line is that sellers need to make sure they do not misrepresent their property and that they provide the proper disclosures required in their area. Seller disclosures can be obtained from your real estate team or directly from the Internet (be sure you are familiar with the laws for disclosure in your area). Sellers also should be familiar with fair housing laws and make sure they do not discriminate against any potential buyers. Contact HUD's Housing Discrimination Hot Line at 800-669-9777.

It is also a good idea to only show the home by appointment and make sure you never show the home when you are home alone. Even sellers that list with brokers have people knock on their door or catch them outside doing yard work and sometimes invite them in to look at their home. After all, who can resist a live buyer?! Contact your local law enforcement organization and tell them you will be putting your home on the market. Ask if they have someone who could visit with you to recommend safety procedures.

Friendly relationships between FSBO's and real estate agents can exist and be productive for both parties. This approach requires an open mind by the FSBO and a sincere belief by the agent that sellers have the right to try to sell their own homes if that is what they want to do.

Buyers and sellers of FSBO properties should make sure they keep the relationship on a professional basis, at least until after closing. Buyers should always hire a professional inspection company to thoroughly inspect the property inside and out. The opportunities in real estate are endless. If everyone involved will keep an open mind and be willing to change paradigms they may have, everyone can profit.

CHAPTER SIX

You *Can* Avoid Foreclosure

Congratulations! You are now a homeowner. You own a piece of the American dream. The most important thing you can do now is to recognize that your monthly house payment should be your first priority. Unfortunately this is not always the case. You now have to make a commitment to take personal responsibility for your financial welfare and to understand that your home is an important financial consideration. After reading this chapter you will be able to

- take proactive steps to avoid foreclosure and ensure financial success and freedom for you and your family.

- avoid unethical companies that offer to buy your home without actually removing you from responsibility for your loan.

- know who to call if you have difficulty managing your debt.

The Mortgage Bankers Association of America estimates that nearly 250,000 homes go into foreclosure annually. This is a problem for all price ranges and all income brackets.

Why after all the time, effort, and money invested in finding just the right home and obtaining a mortgage, can so many people be losing their homes to foreclosure? The following statistics may help answer that question:

- In a George Gallup survey, four groups of people from diverse income groups were asked if they felt they needed more income to make ends meet and, if so, how much. Respondents from every group, earning from $15,000 annually to $150,000, responded that they needed about 10 percent more income to meet their budgets.

- The upper-middle class is characterized by lack of time, financial worries, and lots of stress. Six-figure incomes no longer guarantee comfortable lives. A large part of the upper-middle class are cash poor and under a lot of pressure.

- Four out of five families are strapped with serious money problems.

- An American Bar Association statistic indicates that 89 percent of all divorces are related to financial problems. These marriage tragedies are not caused by lack of money, but rather by the mismanagement of personal finances.

- Money is the #1 cause of stress in America.

- Payments on debt now account for 92 percent of family disposable income.

- In an interview with *Financial Security Digest*, Venita Vancaspel, a financial expert, stated, ". . . of every 100 people who reach age 65 in our country, only 2 are financially independent, 23 must continue to work, and 75 are dependent on friends, relatives, or charity. This means that 98 percent of us are flat broke."

These statistics tell us that most people tend to spend according to their checkbooks and credit card limit.

FORECLOSURE

If you fall behind on your monthly mortgage payment, the lender has the right to foreclose on the loan. You will be forced to move out and then the lender will sell your home to pay off the loan. Legal fees may be added to what you owe and you could lose everything you have invested in your home.

In some states, if the sale does not bring enough to cover your outstanding loan balance and legal fees, the lender may have the right to obtain a deficiency judgment and require you to repay all outstanding balances.

Effects of Foreclosure

Nearly a century and a half ago, author and poet Walt Whitman said, "A man is not a whole and complete man unless he owns a house and the ground it stands on."

If this is true, what kind of impact does it have on families that lose the home they worked so hard for? Again, the following statistics can help answer that for us:

- Money is the #1 cause of stress today.

- The American Medical Association has projected that 75 percent of all doctor visits are stress-related.

- According to psychiatrist David Trachtenberg of Bethesda, Maryland, "Stress threatens people's sense of self-worth and mastery, leading to depression, loss of energy, loss of focus, and disinterest in sex."

- According to *Money Madness,* 90 percent of all crime is committed for money.

It is critical for all of us to understand the impact foreclosures have, not just on families, but also on communities and on the workplace. We should work together to reduce the number of foreclosures in America. One of the ways we can do this is through education *before* and *after* a home is purchased. Study the steps for avoiding foreclosure that follow and share them with anyone who may need them. Together we can avoid foreclosure!

Four Steps to Avoid Foreclosure

You can decrease the possibility for foreclosure by following these four steps:

1. Create a realistic spending plan.

2. Ask for help.

3. Negotiate your debts.

4. Sell your home before foreclosure.

Step 1: Create a Realistic Spending Plan

The first step is to *create a realistic spending plan.* For most of us that is easier said than done. Part of the problem is that we resist "budgeting" because it is a painful event. Anthony Robbins, one of the most successful motivational and educational speakers in America, says that ". . . we spend our time in one of two ways, avoiding pain or seeking pleasure."

If it is true that most of us spend according to our checkbooks, then developing a budget may seem like a painful and limiting way to live. That is why the first step is to create a spending plan, not a budget. Shellie and Jon Black, authors of a money management program, define financial freedom as, "Freedom from worry, anxiety, stress, and relationship problems due to money." That is a goal worth working for!

❗ BEWARE

● When creating your spending plan, make sure you take into consideration the affect your *escrow account* has on your monthly house payment. Your escrow account is the amount of your monthly payment that pays for your property taxes and insurance.

Many people fail to take into consideration that taxes and insurance can increase, even while your principal and interest payment may remain the same. This means that even if you have a fixed-rate mortgage your payment still can increase due to raises in taxes and insurance payments. Consult with local real estate agents and your lender to get a feel for how much taxes and insurance typically increase each year.

It may be helpful to create a savings for your home category to which you contribute a certain amount to each month. Then, if your escrow account does go up at the beginning of the next year, you have the money in your budget to cover the increase.

Lenders usually reevaluate escrow accounts at the beginning or the end of each year to make sure they are collecting enough money to pay the taxes and insurance when it becomes due. If they determine there will be a shortage, they usually will raise your monthly payment to make up the difference. For many people who live paycheck to paycheck, this increase can cause them to lose their home to foreclosure. Take the Cunningham's, for instance:

Mark and Janey Cunningham finally had moved into their dream home. The sales price was a little higher than they had planned to pay, $175,000, but they were able to scrape up a 20 percent down payment for a loan amount of $140,000 and still pay their closing costs. They were fine the first year, although they did not put much money into savings due to all the new things they wanted for their new home.

In February of the second year, they received a notice from their lender that their payments were going up $328 per month to cover the shortage in their escrow account. They had no idea where the $328 was supposed to come from. When the March payment became due, they did not have the money for the higher payment, so they did not send it in. They were hoping to come up with a solution. Instead, Janey's car had to have new tires, the air-conditioning system on the house needed repair, and Mark's unscheduled business trip required him to purchase new clothes.

Guess what happened when the April payment was due? Like most people, Mark and Janey spend according to what's in their checking accounts. The only problem was that their checking account had had the money for their March house payment in it because they did not send it in due to the higher payments. They had spent it during March.

Now they were not only short the March payment, but had no way to make the April payment. To top it off, there were now late charges added to the March payment.

The Cunninghams did not know where to turn. They kept hoping a miracle would happen and they would find a way to catch up. Unfortunately, the Cunninghams waited too long to put their home on the market and could not get it sold before it was foreclosed. They lost all of the money they had put down, their closing costs, and the improvements they had made to the property.

What could the Cunninghams have done that may have saved their home? As soon as the Cunninghams received the notice stating their payment was going to increase, they should have contacted their lender and asked for an explanation. After they understood why the payment was going up, they should have informed the lender of the problem it was going to cause with their spending plan and asked if there were any options to solve the problem.

The lender may have allowed the escrow account on the loan to be dropped and for the Cunninghams to be responsible for paying their own taxes and insurance. They had put 20 percent down on the loan and some lenders will allow borrowers with a 20 percent or more down payment to do this.

This would allow the Cunninghams to keep the same monthly payment that they were comfortable with. That would give them time to find a way to pay their taxes and insurance each year. Options that may help include:

- Finding a second part-time job until the amount they needed was in savings.

- Talking to their employers about a raise.

- Talking to an accountant about how much of a refund they could expect from the IRS.

- Seeing if they could claim more deductions so that they would get more money back each month.

The point is that you have to build into your spending plan enough money to cover the rising cost of home ownership. Fannie Mae states that some financial advisors also recommend you save approximately 1 percent of the purchase price of the house for annual maintenance and repairs.

Step 2: Ask for Help

The second step to take if you do miss even one payment is to *ask for help* right away! According to Fannie Mae, even one payment can be difficult to make up. Gene Eisman, with Fannie Mae public relations, states, "When a home is foreclosed nobody wins. Not the lender, the servicer, Fannie Mae, and certainly not the home owner."

Fannie Mae has put a procedure in place to help people remain in their homes if they have financial problems that endanger their ability to pay their mortgages. It feels the last and least-desirable option is foreclosure.

Fannie Mae requires that all lenders and servicers (companies you actually make your payments to) that work with it has a *workout plan.*

If a mortgage falls into serious delinquency, usually 90 days or more, the servicer is required to use one of the following options as a workout plan to reduce the possibility of foreclosure:

- *Temporary forbearance.* A payment plan that would allow the payments to be made up over time. For example, in addition to the full monthly payment, the mortgagee would pay 20 percent of the arrears until it is paid off. This is the preferred method and Gene Eisman of Fannie Mae public relations states that three out of four mortgagees using this method successfully avoid foreclosure.

- *Loan modification.* The terms of the loan may be modified; for example, interest rate reduced, type of loan modified, term of loan modified, etc.

- *Preforeclosure sale.* An option for borrowers who are unable to work with the first two options. With a preforeclosure sale, Fannie Mae agrees to accept a short payoff if the home does not sell for enough to cover the mortgage and a foreclosure is prevented. This means a foreclosure will not be on borrowers' credit report and can go a long way to helping them get back on their feet financially.

The key to the workout plan is that the borrower has to notify the servicer immediately and tell it:

- Your payment is overdue.

- Why you have been unable to make the payment.

- When and if you expect the situation to change.

This needs to be followed up with a letter containing the following information:

- Your name

- Your loan number

- Your property address

- Your daytime and evening phone numbers

- Brief explanation of why you cannot make payment

The lender is more likely to work with you if you have had a good payment record in the past, you are sincere in wanting to make the payments, and you contacted them instead of them having to track you down.

If you find you can no longer afford the payments on your home, contact a real estate professional and possibly an attorney as soon as possible. A real estate professional even may be able to find an investor interested in purchasing your house and leasing it back to you. If you have a large equity, you may be able to find an investor who is willing to help you make up back payments for a share in the equity when you do sell the house. The more people you have working to help you find a solution, the better your chances of avoiding foreclosure and losing everything.

❗ BEWARE

There are unethical companies and individuals who prey on those in financial difficulty. One type of "distressed homeowner" program has the "buyer" being paid a fee to have the title transferred to it. Then it turns around and sells it. It falsely tells the homeowners that transferring the title to a third party allows them to walk away from the mortgage.

Step 3: Negotiate Your Debts

The third step is to try to negotiate your debts with your other creditors *before* you jeopardize your home. There are several nonprofit consumer agencies available to help people in financial difficulty to negotiate their debts with creditors and develop budgets. Two of the most popular are:

- Consumer Credit Counseling Service (CCCS) at 800-308-3199.

- Credit Counseling Centers of America (CCA) at 800-493-2222 or on the Internet at www.cccamerica.org

To find out if there are other counseling agencies in your community, you also can contact the Fannie Mae HomePath Hotline at 800-732-6643.

Many of these agencies have access to a Fannie Mae software product called Desktop Home Counselor®. Desktop Home Counselor has a budget feature that will help you and the counselor work through the details of tracking your monthly expenses and of setting up a workable spending plan.

Be sure to ask counseling services:

- What fees they charge

- How the fees are financed (when they must be paid)

Nancy Johnson, president and CEO of CCCS in California, states:

> The majority of our funding comes from creditors, which is a percentage of the money we send them under debt management payments. We charge our clients up to $20 a month for our services.

Many people wait until they are two or three or more mortgage payments behind before they do anything. Most of the time it is because they are hoping either that they can "catch up" next month—like the Cunninghams were—or they are so confused and scared they do not know what to do. The sooner you apply these three steps to avoiding foreclosure, the less likely you are to lose your home.

❗ Beware

Some consumers have reported that mortgage lenders look at the CCCS program the same way as having filed bankruptcy. If you are in the market for a new home and are considering working with a counseling program or filing bankruptcy, you may want to discuss your situation with a lender and an attorney to see which one makes the most sense for you.

Most lenders will want to see that it has been at least two years since the bankruptcy was discharged and also may apply the same two-year standard to the date you complete your counseling program. If your time frame is less than that, it does not mean you cannot obtain a mortgage. It just means you probably will be charged higher rates and fees.

Also, do not confuse these community-based counseling services with so-called "credit doctors" who promise to "fix" your bad credit record for a fee. It cannot be done. The only real answer is to accept responsibility for creating your own financial freedom by developing a realistic spending plan and then holding yourself accountable on a day-to-day basis. The rewards are worth it!

Step 4: Sell Your Home before Foreclosure

If all else fails let your lender know you are going to sell your home as soon as possible. This is a good time to have a good real estate service team in place. Let them know your situation and have them help you position your home for a fast closing. Make sure they use the finance incentives discussed in this book to open up the market to as many buyers as possible.

Have the real estate agent on your team contact your lender and find out exactly how much time you have. When the agent communicates with the lender, it shows you are serious about trying to resolve the situation and they may give you more time. The key is good communication between you, your lender, and your team.

SUMMARY

Losing your home to foreclosure can be a devastating experience that can be emotionally trying for homeowners. If you use the following four steps to avoid foreclosure you can reduce the possibility of it happening to your family:

1. Create a realistic spending plan.

2. Ask for help.

3. Negotiate your debts.

4. Sell your home before foreclosure.

Step 1 is to create a realistic spending plan. You should consider taking the time to do this as soon as you are prequalified by a real estate professional. Once you know the price range and monthly payment the lender will allow, you can prepare a spending plan that would include a housing category for possible escrow account increases and one for maintenance and emergencies. If you find that your income will not allow you to save in these categories, you may want to adjust the price range for the home you want to buy.

Step 2 is to not be afraid to ask for help as soon as possible. Contact your servicer (company you make payments to) immediately and try to work out a plan that will give you an option you can be comfortable with. You also may want to see if your real estate team has any options that will work for you.

Step 3 is to try to negotiate your debts with your other creditors. A counseling service may help you negotiate reduced monthly payments. You also can receive counseling from local nonprofit associations that will help you develop a budget.

Home ownership is known as the American dream. Make sure you take the time and effort to protect your dream and your family from foreclosure. Ask your real estate professional about seminars that may be available in your area to help you make educated decisions about home ownership.

If all else fails, proceed to Step 4 and let your lender and your agent know you plan to sell your home.

CHAPTER SEVEN

To Refinance or Not to Refinance?

The purpose of this chapter is to give you information to consider before you decide if refinancing is right for you. When interest rates drop, homeowners seem to get caught up in a refinancing frenzy without always considering the costs involved or other options that may be better for them. All too often people refinance only to put their home on the market a year or two later. The result is that they end up walking away with less equity than they could have if they had not been so quick to refinance. After reading this chapter, you will

- have options to consider before you get ripped off by choosing a refinance option that is not in your best interest.

- be able to save money on closing costs when you refinance.

- know how to lower your interest rate on some loan programs without having to requalify (have credit checked or income and debt analyzed for the loan).

There are varied opinions on the right way and the wrong way to refinance. Some people will tell you that it only makes sense to refinance if your new rate will be at least 2 percent lower than the old one. Others will tell you that if you can recoup the refinance charges within 14 to 18 months, it is a good deal.

The truth of the matter is that what makes sense for one person may not make sense for another. The following questions may help you decide if refinancing is right for you:

- How will refinancing affect your tax situation?

- What type of loan do you currently have?

- How many years do you have left on your current loan?

- How many years and how much interest will you be adding if you refinance?

- How much will you be reducing your payments?

- If you have a VA loan, are you the original borrower?

- Can you obtain a rate reduction instead of refinancing?

- What is your purpose for refinancing?

- How long do you plan to remain in your home?

- If you plan to move in the near future, how does the cost of refinancing compare with the cost of moving now?

- How much will your refinancing costs be?

- How long will it take you to recoup the refinancing costs with the money you save from refinancing?

The bottom line is that you want to know how much interest you will save, how much refinancing is going to cost, and how long it will take to get your money back. These may just be a few of the questions you will want to consider, but this should give you a good place to start.

You also can get a lot of good information from the Internet. Microsoft's HomeAdvisor and Quicken Mortgage, to name just a couple, have sites that have a section with valuable information on refinancing. Most Internet sites have a handy form you can fill out right on the computer to get a calculation of how long you need to remain in your home before you will break even on the refinancing cost. You can access HomeAdvisor at www.HomeAdvisor.com and Quicken Mortgage at www.Quicken.com.

The sample refinance worksheet will help you calculate a refinance.

Just remember that financial information is only one aspect of the question. Only you can answer if refinancing makes sense for you on a personal level. A good real estate team can help make sure you have considered all of your options before making a decision. You may find that your best option is to move into the dream home you have been wanting instead of refinancing your current one.

WHEN DOES IT PAY TO REFINANCE?

These three questions will help you answer this question:

1. How much will your payments be lowered?

2. How much will it cost to refinance?

3. How long do you plan to keep the home?

The key to making a refinance pay off is to make sure you stay in the home at least long enough to recover the costs. This worksheet will help you estimate how long it will take before refinancing begins to pay off.

> Example: Loan Amount—$100,000
> New Interest Rate—7%   Old Rate—8.75%

(continued)

Estimated Refinancing Costs		*Additional Costs You May Need to Pay:*	
Discount points	$ 0		
Origination fee	1,000	**Prepaid Expenses***	
Appraisal	225	Interest**	_____
Credit report	50	Hazard insurance	_____
Flood certification fee	17	Home insurance	_____
Processing fee	_____	Mortgage insurance	_____
Document prep fee	_____	Property taxes	_____
Underwriting fee	134	**Total prepaids**	_____
Escrow waiver fee	_____		
Tax service fee	71		
Closing fee	100		
Title insurance	200		
Recording fees	32		
Survey	_____		
Pest inspection	_____		
Other (prepayment penalties, courier fees, etc.)	_____		
Total closing costs (A)	**$1,829**		

Complete formula:

A. Total closing costs $1,829
B. New monthly PITI   786
C. Current monthly PITI payment   665
D. Difference between **B** & **C**   121

A (Total costs) ÷ D (Difference in payments)
= Number of months to recoup costs

$1,829 ÷ $121 = 15 months

Calculating Your Refinance Costs and Savings

For those of you who like to work with numbers, consider a typical example. Sam owes $130,000 on his first lien. He has a swimming pool that he owes another $16,000 on. The first lien has an interest rate of 7.625 percent with 23 years remaining, and the second lien has a rate of 8.5 percent with 9 years remaining.

First, look at the interest costs. On a $130,000 balance at 7.625 percent, his interest cost is approximately $9,900 per year. A $16,000 loan at 8.5 percent will cost him around $1,360 per year. The total interest costs are $11,260 per year. If he refinanced both liens into one 30-year loan, he could get a rate of 6.625 percent. That would give him a yearly interest cost of around $9,673. He would have a pretax savings of $1,587. Sounds pretty good so far, correct?

Now let us look at what it is going to cost him. A good rule of thumb in some states is to estimate 4 percent for closing costs. The costs go down a bit if your current loan is less than three years old, but the costs do not vary a great deal. His cost is going to be around $5,840. He can pay for this out of pocket, or he can add it into his loan. Either way, it is still money that he is going to spend now or when he pays off the loan.

Just because you are adding in the refinancing costs to your mortgage does not mean you do not pay it back. Before taxes, it will take 3.68 years to recoup his costs. If we assume that he will get a tax deduction of $444 on the $1,587, which would be 28 percent, then he is only saving $114. Now it really takes him 5.11 years to recoup his costs. But let us not forget the origination fee is deductible and he would get a tax deduction on that of $408. So the real cost to close would be about $5,072 and the real savings would be around $1,143, so it would take him 4.44 years to recoup his costs to refinance.

There is one more thing to consider: What could he do with his money if he did not spend it on the refinance? Let us assume he can get an average annual return on his money of 7 percent and continue to use the same 4.4 years. $5,480 invested at an average return of 7 percent will make him about $384 per year. Yearly savings then become $1,143 minus $384 or around $760. Now it will take 6.67 years to recoup costs.

Streamlining Your FHA (Federal Housing Administration) Loan

Okay, by now you are probably thinking, "Good Grief! That is way too complicated!" It does take some thought, but the premise is easy: Refinance only if you will remain in the home long enough to recoup the cost of refinancing.

The following real-life situation will show you the impact of knowing your options:

Rondah-Lyn, a local real estate agent, was having her teeth cleaned. Chelsea, the dental hygienist, was a young woman with two children who was going through a divorce. She did not want to add more trauma to her children by having to move them from their home and school.

Chelsea was telling Rondah-Lyn about the problems she had trying to refinance her home. Five weeks ago she had applied to a lender to refinance her home and lower her payments. After paying $350 for an appraisal, $85 for a credit report, and $125 for an application fee, the loan officer told her she did not qualify for the rate and fees he first quoted her without her ex-husband's income.

Refinancing it would cost her more than she could afford. He recommended she ask her parents or her ex-husband for the extra money! She was devastated.

The good news is that now Chelsea was talking to the right person! Rondah-Lyn asked her what kind of loan she currently had on her home. It was an FHA loan. That is all Rondah-Lyn had to hear! She showed her how she could streamline an FHA loan without having to qualify for or incur all the expenses of a full refinance.

You see, FHA allows loans to be streamlined to reduce the monthly payment when interest rates decrease. To top that off, they do not require a credit report, income verification, or (in some cases) an appraisal. They even will allow the settlement fees from the closing agent to be rolled into the loan amount so the borrower does not have to come up with money out of pocket.

The lender Chelsea went to should have immediately told her about streamlining instead of refinancing and not put her through five weeks of stress and then rejection. FHA recognizes that if payments can be decreased, there is less likelihood of the loan going into foreclosure. So they allow all FHA loans to be streamlined. The borrower can streamline with the current lender or, if the payments have been current, with any lender.

The obvious question is, "Why did the loan officer Chelsea was working with not offer the streamline?" The answer to that is because loan officers fall into one of three categories:

1. Those who are ethical, experienced, and know what they are doing.

2. Those who are unethical and take advantage of consumers.

3. Those who do not have a clue what they are doing!

The loan officer obviously fell into one of the last two categories. Having a good real estate team in place is not just for when you want to buy or sell real estate. You need to have a team you can count on for all of your real estate needs. It is important to find a team that knows the value of long-term relationships with its customers.

In the situation above, Rondah-Lyn did not make a commission from helping the hygienist streamline. But she did add a customer for life! The agent received many referrals from the hygienist when others heard about how knowledgeable the agent was. You see, finance really is the key to buying, selling, and owning real estate!

VA loans allow a similar process called VA rate reduction. The catch here is that the original veteran is the only one who can obtain a rate reduction. If you assume a VA loan and want to lower the rate, you will need to refinance.

Streamlining can make a difference to a lot of borrowers. Many people get rejected when trying to refinance because their debt situation has changed. When you refinance, most lenders will look at ratios the same way they do when you purchase. If you have added debt, gotten divorced, filed bankruptcy, changed jobs, or had credit problems, you still can streamline if your original loan is an FHA loan.

Remember, all FHA lenders can streamline, but some may not be willing to take the time or may charge more than others. Your team should be able to help you streamline with little or no qualifying and no cost.

The FHA Streamline Refinance Guidelines will help you determine if streamlining will work for you.

FHA STREAMLINE REFINANCE GUIDELINES

- *Eligible properties.* Owner-occupied, primary residence, one to four units, second or investor homes.

- *Loan Term.* Lesser of 30 years, or the unexpired term plus 12 years rounded down to nearest 5-year increment. A 30-year can be reduced to 15-year; payments cannot increase more than $50.

- *LTV.* There are no loan-to-value ratio (LTV) requirements on a streamline without an appraisal.

- *Maximum loan amount.* No cash out. The new mortgage cannot exceed the existing principal balance. No interest can be included in the new loan. With an appraisal, you can roll in closing costs.

- *Underwriting.* No qualifications required by HUD. Lenders may impose their own guidelines, such as verification of deposit to see that borrower has two months' house payments, or verification of employment to see that borrower is employed, or 12-month pay history on loan. All borrowers must have been on title for at least six months before they can streamline. The only exception is if the borrower receives title by inheritance, divorce, or death. Principal and interest (P&I) must be lower than the current payment, unless the term is reduced from a 30-year to a 15-year (maximum $50 increase). An ARM can be streamlined if the new fixed-rate loan is no more than 2 percent higher than the current ARM rate. If streamline is from ARM to ARM, the new rate also must be at least 2 percent below current rate.

- *Assumability.* Can be assumed by a qualified buyer for the life of the loan.

- *MIP.* One-time and monthly mortgage insurance premiums (MIPs) are required. LTVs for all streamlines without appraisals are to be considered less than 90 percent for purposes of determining term on monthly MIP. Condos require monthly MIP only. One-time MIP may be included in the loan amount or paid in cash. Financed MIP on the old loan will be credited back to the old loan, then the new MIP will be added to the new loan if the loan is less than seven years old.

- *Buydowns.* Not allowed on streamlining.

! Beware

● There are many companies advertising home equity loans or refinancing up to 125 percent of the value of your home. Make sure you have a real estate professional review the loan fees and terms with you before considering these loans.

> Cheri Glass had recently closed on her home. Shortly after, a lender sent a letter in the mail stating that she was "preapproved" for a home equity loan of $25,000. It could be used for anything—swimming pool, new car, new appliances, vacation, anything! A week later, Cheri received a phone call asking if she had received the letter and when did she want to close?
>
> Cheri was not interested, but out of curiosity asked what the interest rate would be, what were the discount points, and how much money would be needed to close. The lender wanted a 15 percent interest rate, 6 points, and another $1,500 in closing costs! When she told them no thanks, they got offended. She told them she could do much better at her bank and then hung up.
>
> The next day she received a call from the loan officer's supervisor. He wanted to know why Cheri refused the loan when she was already approved for it. She told him she did not like his terms and fees. He got insulted and said they had thought they had made her a good offer and could not believe she was not interested. When she told him she could get a much better deal at her bank he just said, "Well, I'm not so sure about that. Is your husband home? Let me talk to him." Cheri just hung up.

The point to this story is that there are a lot of unethical, greedy lenders out there you need to watch out for. Make sure you put a team together that will keep each other accountable for providing you quality service and will help ensure you do not get taken advantage of by lenders like the one just described.

REVERSE MORTGAGES

For homeowners 62 and older, an alternative to refinancing or home equity loans is a reverse mortgage or home equity conversion mortgage. A reverse mortgage is a special type of mortgage that allows you to tap the equity you have in your home. Unlike traditional mortgages, instead of having to make a monthly payment, the payments are made *to* you, against the equity in the house. The payments are reversed. You make no payments until you no longer occupy the house as your principal residence.

There are several types of reverse mortgages available. Make sure you ask the lender for a written estimate of all charges during the life of the reverse mortgage. You may want to discuss your options with your real estate team, your accountant, and possibly a real estate attorney.

Fannie Mae's reverse mortgage is called the Home Keeper Mortgage. After reading this section you can obtain more information about reverse mortgages by contacting your real estate team or by contacting Fannie Mae on the Internet at www.fanniemae.com.

Frequently Asked Questions about Reverse Mortgages

The following commonly asked questions were obtained with permission from Fannie Mae's Web site.

Q: How does a Home Keeper reverse mortgage differ from a home equity loan?

A: With a home equity loan, you must make regular monthly payments to repay the loan. These payments begin as soon as you originate the loan. To qualify for such a loan, you must have a monthly income great enough to make those payments. The Home Keeper reverse mortgage has two principal differences from the typical home equity loan:

1. You do not repay the loan as long as the home remains your principal residence.

2. Your income is not considered when qualifying you for the loan.

Q: Who is eligible for a Home Keeper reverse mortgage?

A: You, and any coborrowers, must be at least 62 years old and either own your own home free and clear or have a very low outstanding mortgage. Your home must be a single-family home or a condominium. Cooperatives are not currently eligible for Home Keeper loans. You also must agree to attend a consumer education session on reverse mortgages.

Q: How much money can I borrow?

A: The maximum amount you can borrow—the principal limit—is based on three factors:

1. The number of borrowers

2. The age of the borrowers

3. The adjusted property value

The adjusted property value is the lesser of the appraised value of the home or the Fannie Mae loan limit (your real estate team can give you the current Fannie Mae loan limits).

Q: How will I receive my money?

A: When you close your loan, you will select one of the following payment plans:

- *Tenure option.* You receive equal monthly payments for as long as you occupy the home as your principal residence.

- *Line of credit option.* You draw on the principal limit of cash available at times and in amounts you choose.

- *Modified tenure option.* You set aside a portion of loan proceeds as a line of credit and receive the rest in the form of equal monthly payments.

Contact your real estate team or the Fannie Mae Web site for examples of the amounts that may be available.

Q: Will I have to pay any fees to obtain a Home Keeper reverse mortgage?

A: Yes, you will pay an origination fee, points, other closing costs, and a monthly servicing fee. You can finance almost all of these fees by including them in your loan balance so that you do not have to pay cash for them.

Q: How is interest charged?

A: The Home Keeper is an adjustable-rate mortgage. The interest rate is tied to the one-month CD index that is published weekly by the Federal Reserve. The rate adjusts monthly and there is no limit to the amount the rate can change at each monthly adjustment. However, over the life of the loan, the rate cannot adjust more than 12 percentage points.

Q: Can I be forced to sell or vacate my home if the money I owe on the loan exceeds the value of my home?

A: No. As long as you continue to occupy the property as your principal residence and abide by the loan agreement, which states that you are responsible for property maintenance and payment of all property taxes and insurance, you can stay in your home as long as you choose. No deficiency judgment may result from your Home Keeper loan.

Q: Will my heirs owe anything to the mortgage lender if I die before the loan is paid off?

A: Upon your death, the loan balance, consisting of payments made to you or on your behalf (such as fees) plus accrued interest, becomes due and payable. Your heirs may repay the loan by selling the home or by paying off the Home Keeper loan so that they may keep the home. If the loan balance exceeds the value of your property, your estate will owe no more than the value of the property. No additional financial claims may be made against your heirs or estate.

Q: What if I decide to sell my home?

A: If you choose to sell your home, even to your children, the outstanding loan balance becomes due and payable to the mortgage lender at the time of sale. You would receive any proceeds exceeding the loan balance.

Q: Will funds I receive from a Home Keeper reverse mortgage affect my Social Security, Medicare, Supplemental Security Income (SSI), or Medicaid benefits?

A: Home Keeper loan funds do not affect your Social Security or Medicare benefits because those benefits are not based on the assets of the recipient. However, in the federal Supplemental Security Income program, beneficiaries must keep their liquid resources under certain limits ($2,000 for individuals and $3,000 for couples). If you do not spend Home Keeper advances in the month received, then such funds are considered part of your liquid resources and may adversely affect your eligibility for SSI. Therefore, a Home Keeper borrower who also receives SSI should never draw more money than he or she actually needs that month.

Regulations for state-administered programs such as Medicaid, AFDC, and food stamps, and for state-funded welfare programs (such as state supplements to SSI), all have different eligibility requirements. You should consult your local Area Agency on Aging for these programs to determine how Home Keeper payments may affect your particular situation.

Q: Where can I learn more about the Home Keeper reverse mortgage?

A: You may order a list of participating lenders from Fannie Mae's Consumer Resource Center by contacting 800-7-FANNIE (800-732-6643). You also may request *"Money from Home,"* Fannie Mae's guide to Home Keeper and Home Equity Conversion Mortgages.

To learn more about all types of reverse mortgages, you can write to the American Association of Retired Persons (AARP) to request their guide to converting your home equity into cash. For a free copy, write to: Home Made Money, AARP Home Equity Information Center, 601 E. Street, NW, Washington, DC 20049.

SUMMARY

Many people get caught up in the refinancing craze without considering their options. Make sure you carefully review your options with your real estate team before you refinance. Some of your options may include:

- Being able to sell your home and buy your dream home earlier than you anticipated

- Streamlining a loan instead of refinancing to reduce closing costs (FHA loans allow borrowers to reduce the interest rate with reduced documentation called streamline refinancing. Guidelines vary with different lenders, but you can typically lower your interest rate without an appraisal, credit report, employment or asset verification, or having to meet the income-to-debt ratios usually required. Because this is not a full refinance, the costs are typically lower than a normal refinance.)

- Getting a rate reduction on a VA loan

- Obtaining a reverse mortgage instead of refinancing (Home-owners 62 and older can select a reverse mortgage or a home equity conversion mortgage. These loans allow you to tap the equity you have in your home and receive payments against your equity instead of you having to take out a loan that requires you to make payments on it. The key is that you do not have to repay the loan as long as the house is your principal residence. Several types of reverse mortgages are available. For more information on these types of mortgages you can contact your local lender or visit the Fannie Mae Web site at www.fanniemae.com.)

There are numerous free sources available to you to help you make an educated decision. Some of those include information available on the Internet. If you are considering refinancing, it will be worth your time to check out the Quicken, HomeAdvisor, and Fannie Mae Web sites. The reference section in the back of the book gives you Web site addresses for easy access.

If you do not have access to a computer, you may want to see if your real estate team can do this with you. Your local library also may have no-fee Internet access.

CHAPTER EIGHT

Take Charge!

By now you should be able to see that selling, buying, and owning real estate is a big responsibility and a huge commitment. You have to be willing to accept responsibility for taking charge of your success. If you do not take charge, you set yourself up to be taken advantage of by unethical people in the business. After reading this chapter you will be able to

- take charge of your financial success with real estate.

- compare advantages and disadvantages of one-stop shopping, loans obtained over the Internet, and computerized loan origination systems (CLOs).

- recognize the benefits of working with real estate professionals who have received designations through advanced education.

- know specific steps you can take to become a responsible team member.

Who Is the Best Consumer Advocate for Real Estate?

Who really is the best consumer advocate when it comes to real estate? Is it the real estate agent or the lender? When you stop to think about it the answer is simple. Neither one. The best consumer advocate is the team. Remember the old saying, "The sum of the parts is greater than the whole"? That statement has never been truer than in the case of buying and selling real estate. To increase your chances of a successful closing and to keep more of your own money in your pocket, you need to have a team in place that practices team spirit. A team works in harmony with each other toward a common purpose or goal.

The best consumer advocate will be a team that holds each member accountable for working toward a successful closing for each and every customer. Many lenders are launching "consumer direct" marketing campaigns advocating that consumers come to them first before shopping for a home. That does not sound like such a bad idea until you remember that although there are a lot of ethical lenders, there are also a lot of unethical lenders out there. Who will keep the lender accountable for delivering quality service if a consumer goes directly to the lender? Who will be in charge of reviewing the HUD 1 and making sure the fees at closing match the fees quoted on the original good faith estimate?

Also remember the example at the end of Chapter 2, who will most likely get the best service and the best pricing?

- *Buyer A.* Referred to a lender by an agent who brings the lender a lot of business.

- *Buyer B.* Buyer chooses the lender out of the phone book or off the Internet.

Buyer A will most likely get the best deal because the lender knows that there is someone checking to make sure that customer receives the best service available. In business, volume speaks; if the agent is the one who brings a lot of business to the lender, that agent's customer will be important to the lender, not just another loan.

This is true if the agent is a true professional and intends to make a long-term career out of real estate. Unfortunately, there are unethical agents in the business also. That is why it is so important for consumers to build teams that will hold each other accountable for looking out for the consumer's needs.

You can do this by making a commitment to learn all you can about the steps involved and how to access information to help you stay current. You have already made a good start by reviewing this book. Tools to help you simplify the process are *Microsoft's Home-Advisor, Quicken Mortgage,* and Internet sites such as Mortgage. com. Many of these sites will allow you to shop for interest rates and obtain prequalification with a number of lenders. They also offer a wide variety of useful information about the homebuying process, such as gaining an understanding of the mortgage process, finding the right neighborhood, finding the right home, securing a mortgage, financing, and understanding the offer and closing process.

PROS AND CONS OF INTERNET SERVICES

The Internet is changing our world as we speak, including the real estate industry. It is wonderful that so much information is available. Just make sure you consider all of your options before being lured by the convenience of using an online mortgage company.

Do not get the wrong idea; it is not a bad idea to shop the Internet. If you make sure you take service and integrity into account and make sure you know you will receive the service you need when it counts, you may get a good deal. You may want to compare loans you can get on-line and then see if a local lender can match it. If not, you may want to give obtaining a loan through the Internet a try.

! Beware

● Things you want to consider include making sure you inquire as to what happens if there is a problem at closing. If you or your buyer obtains financing over the Internet, will there be someone available with a vested interest to take care of last minute problems? Or will there be someone in customer service in a remote location who couldn't care less if the loan closes on time? If fees or rates are higher than promised, what are the buyer's options if current market rates are higher than they were when the buyer first made loan application? Are you aware are of all of the loan options and ways to save on closing costs that would be in your best interest? If you have taken the time to study the loan options presented in this book, you will have a better chance of getting the best deal.

There are so many options available these days. The right strategy for one person may be completely wrong for another. It is more important than ever that you know how to take charge of your real estate transactions and make sure you have a team in place to guide you and help you make educated decisions on the options that are right for your situation.

The Internet is a wonderful tool as long as you are aware of the risks you take when you rely on services you receive when using it. The Internet is also a great tool for real estate professionals to use to educate consumers and show you how you can be an active part of the team. Remember, the goal of the team is not just to work together on one transaction. The goal is to build a long-term relationship that is built on trust and accountability.

Sites such as Realtor.com allow consumers to access information about neighborhoods, such as:

- Schools

- Crime

- Demographics (data used to identify size, growth, density, and distribution)

- Home listings (from national real estate companies and leading Multiple Listing Services)

Any time you want to buy, sell, refinance, or invest in real estate, you should be able to turn to your team to guide you through the process with the least amount of time and money invested.

ONE-STOP SHOPPING

Brokers and agents have made an effort to add value to the services they provide by offering what is known as *one-stop shopping*. Recognizing that in today's busy world time is of the essence for most people, real estate brokers have tried to expand services they offer to include those of a settlement service provider.

This means that consumers can obtain just about everything they need involving their transaction through their real estate professional right in the real estate office. In addition to listing and purchasing homes, this could include:

- Obtaining a mortgage

- Ordering the title report and appraisal

- Homeowners insurance

- Home inspections

- Home warranties

- Remodeling services

The list could probably go on and on. The point is that many in the industry recognize that consumers could benefit if the steps involved in buying and selling real estate could be streamlined. Instead of dealing with completely different companies for services needed, the consumer could take care of everything right out of the real estate office.

Sounds simple, right? You are forgetting the amount of money generated by the real estate industry. Everyone wants to control the consumer in the hopes of controlling the business. Many companies are offering one-stop shopping successfully, but it is not as widespread as you would think it would be.

To give you an example of some of the problems, consider the following: In 1992, HUD ruled, "Real estate professionals have the right to provide finance counseling to consumers and to receive a fee for these additional services if it is fully disclosed." As you can imagine, the Mortgage Bankers Association (MBA) did not like this at all. They immediately started disputing this with HUD so the National Association of REALTORS® (NAR) stepped in to defend HUD's ruling. To make a long story short, HUD ratified the ruling again in 1997.

Apparently, the government understands the benefit of having the real estate agent involved in the finance end of the transaction to protect the consumer. The end result is that more and more real estate offices will be able to provide one-stop shopping. As a consumer, you need to be aware of the services available to you and also understand the pros and cons of using the services.

There are many levels of one-stop shopping at this time. Some brokers have in-house lenders in their offices while others choose to offer computerized loan origination services (CLOs).

An in-house lender usually has an affiliated business arrangement (AfBA) with the broker owner of the office. This means the broker receives compensation on loans generated by the office. An on-site loan officer is available to the agents' customers to prequalify and originate loans. This can be a great arrangement as long as the loan officer does not take it for granted that he or she will get loans regardless of the service delivered.

Another problem arises when a broker "locks out" other lenders from calling on the office. Brokers need to remember that competition is good for business, and they can profit more by keeping competition alive and well. Some brokers also have been known to put pressure on the agents to use the services of the in-house lender and this can cause hard feelings and an uncomfortable work environment. If you pick up on this you could (and should) take your business elsewhere.

A CLO is more agent driven and consumer friendly. A CLO is simply a software program a real estate agent can use to counsel consumers on financing by accessing current interest rates, reviewing different loan options, prequalifying, and even completing good faith estimates for different loan programs.

If you choose to obtain a loan from a lender on the system, the real estate agent will receive a CLO operator fee. There can be multiple lenders on the system to ensure quality service.

The goal is to save the real estate agent and the consumer time and money by having this information immediately available instead of having to wait to meet with a loan officer. The idea is not for the real estate agent to take the place of the loan officer, but to be able to provide enough counseling to help the consumer make an educated decision on which lender and loan program may be best for them.

You should be informed about the options available to you, and in most cases, have written disclosures to sign that explain the relationship between the lender and the broker or the agent and the CLO system. The key is giving you options and not *steering* you by insisting you only work with one lender.

Although it is recommended that you work with a real estate service team, that does not mean that the team should not give you options within the team. Real estate agents should have at least three lenders on their team. This keeps the lenders focused on delivering quality service each and every time if they want repeat business from your real estate agent.

BENEFITS OF AGENT DESIGNATIONS TO CONSUMERS

Another way to take charge is to work with real estate agents who have designations. Designations acknowledge experience and expertise in various real estate specialties. Designations are earned by completion of required educational programs and levels of production and experience. A designation demonstrates that an agent has expertise to offer that will optimize your buying and/or selling experience.

Real estate designations can be earned through the Professional Certification Corporation, which is managed and directed by Charles Dahlheimer, through the National Association of REALTORS®, and through several other organizations.

Graduate, REALTOR® Institute (GRI)

The REALTOR® Institute, managed by state real estate associations that are members of the National Association of REALTORS®, offers a continuing education program for REALTORS®. Upon completion of this program, REALTORS® earn the designation Graduate, REALTOR® Institute (GRI).

For more information about the GRI designation or other designations that REALTORS® in your area may have, you can contact the National Association of REALTORS® at www.onerealtorplace.com or call them at 800-874-6500.

Seniors Real Estate Specialist (SRES)

The Senior Advantage Real Estate Program was introduced in California in August of 1997 and to the nation in January of 1998. Tim Corliss, founding director of the Senior Advantage Real Estate Council, is immediate past-president of the California Association of REALTORS® and has been in the real estate business for more than 38 years. He was previously president of the Santa Monica Board of Realtors and the Los Angeles Association of Realtors.

For more information or to locate a Seniors Real Estate Specialist, call 800-500-4564, visit www.seniorsrealestate.com or write to The Senior Advantage Real Estate Council, P.O. Box 1315, Murphys, California 95247.

Certified Finance Specialist

A Certified Finance Specialist (CFS) has received advanced training in residential finance programs and techniques. These team members are uniquely qualified to help consumers buy and sell real estate faster and with less money out of pocket.

CFSs belong to the Residential Financing Council (RFC), a division of the Professional Certification Corporation (PCC), whose purpose is to create a national organization comprised of real estate brokers, agents, and representatives from related industries. The RFC provides a source of ethical, knowledgeable professionals for you to work with.

Under the direction of Charles Dahlheimer, the RFC will provide an ongoing source of professional education and marketing assistance to its membership to keep them up-to-date on the latest financing techniques for consumers.

They also will be kept up-to-date on the latest information that benefits consumers through monthly newsletters, annual conventions, and special RealNet Direct TV programs.

For more information on the CFS designation or a list of designees in your area, you can contact the RFC at www.rfcouncil.com.

Benefits of Working with a CFS Designee

CFSs are dedicated to looking out for the consumers' needs in every real estate transaction. They apply their advanced training to save their customers time and money when buying and selling real estate.

They believe that if they look out for the your needs first, success will take care of itself. Their goal is to build long-term relationships with their customers that will last throughout their careers. This gives them added incentive to provide the highest level of service available in the industry.

The motto for CFSs is, "The only room never full is the room for improvement." With this in mind, they are committed to ongoing education to stay on top of the latest information and techniques that will benefit consumers.

CFS designees recognize the importance of a real estate service team dedicated to guiding their customers through all the steps involved in buying and selling real estate. The team holds each other accountable for providing the highest level of service available anywhere in the industry.

Designees will be held accountable by the RFC through telephone and written surveys to customers and through the *Suggestions & Comments* section of the RFC Web site. If a designee does not live up to the reputation for excellence required, their designation may be suspended or revoked by the RFC.

CONSUMER RESPONSIBILITY

One way to keep from getting ripped off when buying and selling real estate is to take the time to build a team you can count on. When you do this, you become a part of the team. As a member of the team, you have a responsibility to the team and to yourself to make sure you are receiving the highest level of service available.

Ways you can accept responsibility include:

- Review "Questions to Ask Your Team" in Chapter 1.

- Enter the relationship with your team with the attitude that you are building a long-term relationship to help you with all of your real estate needs.

- Refer people whom you know are interested in buying and selling real estate to your team.

- Communicate honestly with your team.

- Let your team know if someone on the team is not meeting your expectations.

- Let your team know what they can expect from you.

- Respond to RFC and NAR surveys on the service delivered by designees so you'll get even better service next time.

- If you are dissatisfied with service from a CFS, report it on the RFC Web site. (This is a key CFS accountability.)

- If dissatisfied with service from a REALTOR®, report it to the NAR.

- If dissatisfied with service from a lender, report it to the Mortgage Bankers Association.

- If you feel your team went "above and beyond" the call of duty to serve you, report it on the RFC Web site and send them testimonials they can use with other customers.

- Ask your team about consumer seminars that are available in your area.

- Review your financing options with your team and ask questions on any areas that do not make sense to you.

- Understand how your credit score affects purchasing power and make sure you obtain preapproval as early as possible.

- Do not forget the "Fifth C" of underwriting—your comfort zone.

- Create a "realistic spending plan" to include the expenses of home ownership.

SUMMARY

Owning your own home has long been considered a part of the American dream. Getting ripped off through lack of knowledge or through unethical people in the business should not be a part of the process. The American dream can become a reality for more Americans if everyone involved in the buying and selling process would practice team spirit and work in harmony with each other for successful closings. Put the information in this book to work for you and enjoy the many benefits of home ownership for years to come!

GLOSSARY

absolute auction An auction where the highest bidder receives the property regardless of the amount of the bid. In other words, the seller does not have right of refusal.

abstract of title A summary of the history of all the recorded proceedings and instruments that affect title of property.

amortization Repayment of a debt of both principal and interest over a set period of time, so that at the end of the period the balance is zero.

appraisal An estimate or opinion of value based on facts available at a given time.

appraiser A person who is educated or trained to determine the estimated value of personal or real property.

APR (annual percentage rate) Includes interest paid the first year and closing costs paid. It is the best way for a buyer to compare different lenders' quotes to see which is most competitive.

ARM (adjustable-rate mortgage) A loan that adjusts periodically according to the cost of funds. Adjustment periods are usually one month, six months, one year, three years, or five years. The buyer chooses the adjustment period at loan application.

balloon note A note that allows partial repayment of the debt and a lump-sum payment that is due at a specified time. Balloon mortgages have a shorter term than traditional loans and lower interest.

biweekly mortgage Repayment of a loan every other week instead of once a month. This results in one extra payment that is made and applied directly to the principal each year. This saves thousands of dollars in interest and pays off the debt early.

buydown A payment made to the lender at closing so that the buyer can reduce the interest rate.

buyer's market Condition in which the number of houses available is much greater than the number of interested buyers.

cap A safety valve on ARMs that protects buyers from payments that increase too much at once. Usually ARMs include an adjustment cap and a lifetime of the loan cap.

caveat emptor Latin for "let the buyer beware." The axiom that one who buys something does so at one's own peril.

community lending products Fannie Mae loans that allow buyers in certain income limits or geographical locations to purchase a home with less money out of pocket than standard conventional loans.

comparables Property used as comparisons when estimating the value of a certain property.

CMA (competitive market analysis) Also called market evaluation. Using comparables to estimate the value of property.

computerized loan origination systems (CLOs) Computer systems that are sometimes available through your real estate agent or in other locations to help you sort through various loan programs available. The CLO operator may charge a fee for these services.

consumer real estate advocate (CRA) Someone who counsels consumers and defends their rights to purchase and sell real estate without getting ripped off.

conventional loans Loans that are not insured or guaranteed by the government.

credit score A number lenders use to predict the degree of risk in making a loan. The number is calculated using your past credit score.

default A breach or nonperformance of the terms of a note or the covenants of a mortgage or deed of trust.

deficiency judgment A judgment that may be sought against a borrower when the sale of a foreclosed property does not provide an amount of money sufficient to cover the balance due on the loan.

delinquent A loan payment that has not been received 30 days after its due date.

demand letter A notice issued to a borrower warning of the imminent danger of foreclosure.

dePuds (deminimus planned unit developments) Condominiums that share common areas, such as parks and pools.

discount points Each discount point equals 1 percent of the loan amount. Points increase the lender's yield so the loan can be made at a lower interest rate.

down payment The difference between the sales price of real estate and the amount of the mortgage loan.

earnest money agreement Also called purchase and sale agreement. A contract between the buyer and seller in which the buyer provides earnest money to show intent to complete the purchase of real property.

escrow account Funds held by a lender for payment of taxes, hazard insurance, mortgage insurance, or homeowners dues.

escrow officer An agent who meets with the buyer and seller to obtain signatures on all documents pertaining to the transfer of real property.

equitable right of redemption A defaulted borrower's right to redeem his or her property during a foreclosure, up to the date of the mortgage foreclosure sale.

expired listing A home that has been listed with a real estate company but did not sell before the listing agreement ended.

FHA (Federal Housing Administration) An agency that insures loans made by lenders under FHA guidelines. Web site www.hud.gov.

FNMA (Federal National Mortgage Association) Nicknamed Fannie Mae, FNMA is a private corporation that buys and sells first mortgages in the secondary market. The originating lender is referred to as the primary market. Web site www.fanniemae.com.

FHLMC (Federal Home Loan Mortgage Corporation) Nicknamed Freddie Mac, it is a federal agency that buys and sells first mortgages in the secondary market. (Conventional loans commonly are referred to as FNMA or FHLMC loans because these are the guidelines the lenders must abide by if they want to sell a conventional loan in the secondary market.)

forbearance An effort made by the lender to offer the borrower a method of, or alternatives to, making a loan current if it is in default.

forbearance agreement A verbal or written agreement that the mortgage company will delay exercising its right to foreclose on a loan as the borrower performs certain agreed-upon terms and conditions.

foreclosure An act to eliminate a borrower's interest in real property, usually due to default on the loan.

FRM (fixed-rate mortgage) A mortgage that stays at the same interest rate for the life of the loan.

funding fee The VA's version of MIP. The VA does not charge mortgage insurance so it collects a funding fee based on the amount of down payment. The fee varies depending on first-time use, subsequent use, Reservist/National Guard, or refinances. Can be paid in cash or financed into the loan amount.

good faith estimate An estimate of buyer's closing costs to be paid at closing.

hard money lender A lender who specializes in making loans to buyers with bad credit or who do not fit standard guidelines.

hazard insurance Casualty insurance for real estate that includes protection against loss from fire, certain natural causes, vandalism, and malicious mischief.

homestead exemption A state statutory exemption that protects homestead property, usually to a set amount, against the attachment rights of creditors. Exemptions for all or part of the property tax also are available in some states. The homeowner may need to record a formal declaration of homestead before receiving tax exemptions in some states.

index A measure of prevailing interest rates. The index is added to the margin to determine a new interest rate at the time of adjustment. If the index increases, the interest rate increases unless an interest rate cap is reached.

interest In relation to mortgages, interest is a charge for borrowing money.

interest rate The percentage of an amount of money that is paid for the use of money for a specified time period. It usually is expressed as an annual percentage.

junk fees Fees lenders charge in addition to the origination fee that are in excess of the charges made by other lenders in the marketplace.

These fees may include: document preparation fees, underwriting fees, application fees, processing fees, or warehousing fees. If these fees seem excessive, you may be able to negotiate them. Some lenders feel these charges are necessary to compensate for loans originated that do not close.

loan officer A person who meets with buyers and takes loan applications.

lock This refers to establishing a fixed interest rate for the buyer. This can be done at loan application or just before closing. If not locked at application, the interest rate is "floating" until the loan is locked. Be sure to get a lock agreement in writing.

lock break An exception to a locked rate. Some lenders offer this feature if a buyer wants to eliminate the risk of rates increasing before closing and wants a lower rate if rates drop. Usually the buyer pays a slightly higher discount for this option.

LPOs (limited practice officers) Escrow officers who are certified to practice law as it relates to escrow.

LTV (loan-to-value ratio) Compares the loan amount to the value of the property. The result of dividing the loan amount by either the sales price or appraised value, whichever is lower. For example, a $90,000 loan amount divided by a $100,000 sales price gives you a 90 percent LTV.

MAI (Member Appraisal Institute) A designation is earned here by an appraiser through education, training, and examination.

margin A premium that a lender charges on an adjustable-rate mortgage. (It is the lender's profit.) Once the margin is specified in the loan papers, it does not change. The margin is added to the index to calculate adjustments to the interest rate.

market evaluation Also called CMA. Estimating the value of property by using comparables.

MIP (mortgage insurance premium) Charged by FHA to offset cost of a possible default. This one-time charge can be added to the loan amount or paid in cash at closing. You also have a monthly MIP added to the payment.

mortgage A pledge or security for the payment of a debt.

mortgage banker A company that provides funds for mortgages by using its own funds rather than merely bringing buyer and investor together.

mortgage broker A company that originates loans by bringing buyers and mortgage bankers or investors together. Brokers do not use their own funds.

mortgagee The institution, group, or individual that lends money on the security of pledged real estate.

mortgagor The owner of real estate who pledges property as security for the repayment of a debt; the borrower.

NAR The National Association of REALTORS® is a national organization whose purpose is to encourage professionalism in real estate activities.

negative amortization The increase in the balance of a loan due to unpaid interest being added to the loan balance. Usually occurs on ARMs that have payment caps. The payment cap limits the payment from increasing even though the interest may increase. If the payment is not enough to cover the increased interest payment, the interest for that period is added to the loan balance.

note rate The interest rate on the loan.

origination fee Fee charged by a lender to originate loans.

overages Amount of discount charged over the amount the lending institution requires.

par The principal amount of a mortgage with no premium or discount (100 percent).

PITI Acronym for principal, interest, taxes, and insurance.

PMI (private mortgage insurance) Insurance charged on conventional loans with less than 20 percent down to pay costs in case of default on the loan.

points An amount equal to 1 percent of the principal amount of a loan. Loan discount points are a one-time charge assessed at closing by the lender to increase the yield on the loan to a competitive position with other types of investments. (Also referred to as discount points.)

portfolio A lender's ability to keep a loan "in-house" so that it does not have to meet the guidelines of the secondary market. (Not all lenders have this ability; check with your team.)

premium pricing An option for buyers who are short on cash or who may only be in the home a few years, which allows them to choose a higher interest rate and have the lender pay a portion of the closing costs.

prepaids Fees for taxes, hazard insurance, PMI, first year's hazard insurance premium, first year's PMI premium, and interest from day of closing to end of the month. Prepaids are collected by the escrow reserve lender.

primary market The primary mortgage market lenders that originate loans and usually sell them in the secondary market. This could include institutional lenders such as banks, savings and loans, mortgage bankers, and brokers.

processor The person who sends out verifications for the loan; orders the credit report, appraisal, and title; sets up escrow; and, when the verifications are in, submits the loan to the underwriter for approval.

purchase and sales agreement Also called earnest money agreement. A contract between the buyer and seller in which the buyer provides earnest money to show intent to complete the purchase of real property.

ratios Percentages used by lenders to determine whether a buyer can qualify for a payment. Percentages are determined by comparing debt to income.

REALTOR® A real estate professional who is a member of the National Association of REALTORS® and abides by their code of ethics (a statement of principles that concern the behavior of members).

RESPA The Real Estate Settlement Procedures Act was designed to help homebuyers compare settlement costs among lenders and to prevent kickbacks for referral of business.

secondary market A market where mortgages are bought and sold. Fannie Mae is the largest purchaser in the secondary market.

seller's market When the demand for houses outnumbers the houses available on the market.

streamline refinance Process by which FHA and VA loans reduce the interest rate or term without cost or qualifying. However, some lenders may impose additional requirements for this.

SRPA (Senior Real Property Appraiser) This designation shows that an appraiser is qualified to appraise residential and income-producing property.

table funding The practice in some states of allowing a closing agent in a real estate transaction to fund the loan and allow all parties to receive their funds when they meet to sign the papers for closing.

title Legal evidence of right of possession of land.

title insurance Insurance that protects against defects in title to a specific piece of real property.

underwriter Employee of the lender who determines the degree of risk involved in making a loan. The underwriter approves or rejects the loan.

VA (Department of Veterans Affairs) A government agency that guarantees a portion of a loan for a veteran so lenders will make loans with little or no down payment.

yield The effective rate of return on an investment based on the fees, the rate of interest, and the price paid for the mortgage.

Zachary Taylor Boyd My son; proof that miracles happen!

RESOURCES

American Association of Retired Persons (AARP)
Home Made Money
AARP Home Equity Information Center
601 E. St., NW
Washington, DC 20049
800-424-3410
- Free Guide for turning home equity into cash

Calculated Industries
4840 Hytech Dr.
Carson City, NV 89706
800-854-8075 x 269
www.calculated.com
- Real Estate Master QPIIx Calculator Kit
   Calculator - Instruction Video - Workbook

Consumer Credit Counseling Service (CCCS)
800-308-3199
- Look in your phone book under Credit for
   a location near you.

Credit Counseling Centers of America (CCA)
800-493-2222
www.cccamerica.org
- Look in your phone book under Credit for
   location near you.

Fannie Mae
800-7-FANNIE
www.fanniemae.com
- Homeowner education
- Credit counseling
- Reverse mortgages *(Money from Home Guide)*

Habitat for Humanity
www.habitat.org

Homebid
8700 N. Gainey Center Dr. Suite 150
Scottsdale, ZA 85258
877-2HOMEBID
email: support@homebid.com

Microsoft's HomeAdvisor
www.homeadvisor.com

Mortgage Bankers Association
202-861-6555
www.mbaa.org

National Association of REALTORS®
800-874-6500 Customer Service
www.realtor.com

Nehemiah Program
www.nehemiahprogram.org

NorthStar Direct, Inc.
800-450-4580

Quicken Mortgage
www.quicken.com

Residential Financing Council (RFC)
Charles Dahlheimer, President
314-664-8552
www.rfcouncil.com

**U.S. Department of Housing & Urban
Development (HUD)**
www.hud.gov

CREDIT BUREAU INFORMATION

Equifax Information Services
P.O. Box 740256
Atlanta, Georgia 30374-0241
800-378-2732

Trans Union Corporation
P.O. Box 390
Sprintfield, PA 19064-0390
800-567-5470
800-916-8800

Experian
National Consumer Assistance Center
P.O. Box 949
Allen, TX 75013-0949
800-EXPERIAN

Follow-up with a letter that includes:

- Your full name: first, middle, and last; include Jr., Sr., II, etc.

- Your complete mailing address

- Your date of birth

- Your Social Security number

- Name and account number of the creditor and item disputed

- Specific reason for your disagreement with disputed item

- Your signature

PRINCIPAL AND INTEREST ESTIMATOR

This chart will help you estimate what your house will cost monthly and calculates the approximate monthly mortgage payments of principal and interest, based on your mortgage amount and interest rate. Estimates are based on a 30-year term. If your mortgage falls between the amounts listed, add the figure from the $5,000 column to the lesser amount's figure. These estimates only include principal and interest. Your monthly payment may also include taxes, insurance, mortgage insurance, and homeowners association dues.

You can also visit Web sites on the Internet for these calculations. One site you may want to visit for mortgage payments, free credit reports, amortization schedules, and market updates is Home Loan Corporation at www.homeloancorp.com.

Loan Amount	6%	6. 5%	7%	7. 5%	8%	8.5%
$ 5,000	30	32	33	35	37	38
$ 60,000	360	379	399	420	440	462
$ 80,000	480	506	532	560	587	615
$100,000	600	632	665	699	734	769
$120,000	719	758	798	839	880	923
$140,000	839	885	931	979	1,027	1,076
$160,000	959	1,011	1,064	1,119	1,174	1,230
$180,000	1,029	1,138	1,198	1,259	1,321	1,384
$200,000	1,199	1,264	1,331	1,398	1,468	1,538
$220,000	1,319	1,391	1,464	1,538	1,614	1,692
$240,000	1,439	1,517	1,597	1,678	1,761	1,845
$260,000	1,559	1,643	1,730	1,818	1,908	1,999
$280,000	1,679	1,770	1,863	1,958	2,055	2,153
$300,000	1,799	1,896	1,996	2,098	2,201	2,307

Loan Amount	9%	9. 5%	10%	10. 5%	11%
$ 5,000	40	42	44	46	48
$ 60,000	483	505	529	549	572
$ 80,000	644	673	702	732	762
$100,000	805	841	878	915	952
$120,000	966	1,009	1,058	1,098	1,143
$140,000	1,126	1,177	1,229	1,281	1,333
$160,000	1,287	1,345	1,404	1,464	1,524
$180,000	1,448	1,514	1,580	1,647	1,714
$200,000	1,609	1,682	1,755	1,830	1,905
$220,000	1,770	1,850	1,931	2,012	2,096
$240,000	1,931	2,018	2,106	2,195	2,286
$260,000	2,092	2,186	2,282	2,378	2,476
$280,000	2,253	2,354	2,457	2,561	2,667
$300,000	2,414	2,523	2,633	2,744	2,857

INDEX

About the Authors

Patricia Boyd

Patricia Boyd is a Certified Finance Specialist (CFS). Her goal is to help people own their own home and not get ripped off in the process. And that includes not going into foreclosure. She is CEO and President of RealSeminars, Inc., an education company dedicated to providing *"Real Education to Real People."* She also markets Computerized Loan Origination Systems (CLOs) for Home Loan Corporation.

Boyd received her real estate broker's license at the University of Texas in Arlington. She has been in the real estate and mortgage industry as a top producer since 1980. In 1987, she began educating REALTORS®, loan officers, and underwriters.

Recognizing that finance was a core competency that must be developed for true success in real estate, she wrote and published two books on real estate finance: *Real Accountability in Your Real Estate Team* and *Real Finance: The Key to Listing & Selling Real Estate.* She then developed seminars and created the Certified Finance Specialist (CFS) designation program.

Ms. Boyd went on to team up with Faye Buchholz, Rebekah Petrucci, and Shirley Watson to write and develop two more seminars: *Real Time: Investing in What Really Matters* and *Real Money Management.*

Patricia and Faye have been speakers at the National Association of REALTORS® convention, Century 21® convention, ReMax® of Texas convention, Coldwell Banker® banquets, and many industry gatherings. They also have hosted shows on RealNet Direct TV.

LONNY COFFEY

Lonny Coffey is a mortgage banker. He is an Executive Vice President and Regional Manager for Home Loan Corporation. Home Loan is a nonservicing mortgage banker based in Houston, Texas. His responsibilities include all mortgage loan production, sales, and administration of an operation that closed approximately $185 million in first lien mortgage loans in 1998. Projections for 1999 exceed $200 million. Lonny started the division in May of 1996 and grew the business to become the fourth largest mortgage lender in the Tarrant County, Texas, market in a short 18 months. Lonny believes that communication and customer service are the key to any successful business, and he will tell you that he grew the business the old fashioned way.

Lonny received his BBA in Finance from West Texas State University in 1974 and entered the mortgage loan business the same year. He quickly saw that sales was his strong suit and started originating loans in December of that same year. Lonny is a two-time past president of the Fort Worth Mortgage Bankers Association, has been a member of the board of directors of the Builders Association of Fort Worth and Tarrant County, and was the Chairman of the Board for Housing Opportunities of Fort Worth.

Lonny has been a sales leader in every company he has worked for in loan origination. His best month exceeded $5 million in personal production and in his best year, he closed more than $30 million in first lien mortgages.

Lonny has been a guest speaker at many local and area functions. His expertise lies in mortgage banking, sales, and effective communication.